In the Blood

Critical Histories

David Ludden, Series Editor

A complete list of books in the series
is available from the publisher.

In the Blood

Sickle Cell Anemia and the Politics of Race

Melbourne Tapper

PENN

University of Pennsylvania Press

Philadelphia

10 9 8 7 6 5 4 3 2 1

Published by
University of Pennsylvania Press
Philadelphia, Pennsylvania 19104-4011

Library of Congress Cataloging-in-Publication Data
Tapper, Melbourne.
  In the blood : sickle cell anemia and the politics of race / Melbourne Tapper.
    p.   cm.
  Includes bibliographical references and index.
  ISBN 0-8122-3471-5 (alk. paper)
  1. Sickle cell anemia—Social aspects—United States.   2. Sickle cell anemia—
United States—History—20th century.   3. Afro-Americans—Diseases.   I. Title.
RA645.S53T37   1999
362.1'961527'00973—dc21   98-30061
                                                                          CIP

To
Eskil Emil
and
Haldis Minna

Contents

Introduction   1

1. Interrogating Bodies: When Is a Caucasian Not
a Caucasian?   12

2. An "Anthropathology" of the "American Negro,"
1940–1952   29

3. Medical Problems with Ethnological Solutions:
The Colonial Construction of Sickling in Africa   55

4. Sickling and the Paradoxes of African American
Citizenship   92

Coda   125

Notes   127

Acknowledgments   155

Index   157

Introduction

Sickling (sickle cell trait, a genetic mutation, and sickle cell anemia, the disease that affects persons who inherit the mutated gene from both parents) has been linked to race since James B. Herrick first identified it in a black student from the Caribbean in 1910. The twenty-year-old patient had been studying in Chicago and for about a year had been suffering from pustular lesions and general weakness. After examining the blood of the young man, Herrick believed that he had identified a new disorder, describing it as "anemia with peculiar and elongated red blood cells":

This case is reported because of the unusual blood findings, no duplicate of which I have ever seen described. Whether the blood picture represents merely a freakish poikilocytosis [presence of red blood cells of abnormal, irregular shape] or is dependent on some particular disease, I cannot at present answer. . . . The lesions, as he [the patient] described them, had been pustular, with formation of ulcers and scabs. On healing, scars, many of which he pointed out, were left. Some of the ulcers had been as large as a silver quarter of a dollar. The disease lasted about one year and during this time he had felt somewhat weak and indisposed. . . . The shape of [his] red cells was very irregular, but what especially attracted attention was the large number of thin, elongated, sickle-shaped and crescent-shaped forms. . . . They were surely not artefacts, nor were they any form of parasites.[1]

In 1917, the physician Victor E. Emmel used the techniques of the emerging laboratory-based medicine to establish the authenticity of the cells identified by Herrick and named them "sickle cells."[2] By the early 1920s, the physician Verne Mason coined the term "sickle cell anemia," thus officially establishing Herrick's "peculiar and elongated sickle-shaped cells" as a distinct clinical entity.[3] By the 1930s, sickling had become one of the most intensively studied "hemolytic anemias of childhood" within and outside the United States.[4]

While much of the initial interest in sickling was fueled by a desire to establish a connection between a particular set of clinical symptoms and the presence of peculiarly shaped cells in the blood of the patient, the physicians involved in sickling research very early on started to emphasize the racial specificity of the phenomenon, establishing it as a marker or a symptom of race depending on the context and, implicitly, as a means for assigning racial identity.

In the mid-1970s the physician Richard Williams coined the phrase "black-related diseases" to indicate "not only those illnesses to which Blacks are particularly prone, but also those conditions to which Blacks manifest an unusually severe or idiosyncratic reaction."[5] The most familiar and celebrated of these diseases is arguably sickle cell anemia. An overwhelming number of people with sickling in the United States are of African descent, and the phenomenon occurs among Africans living in Africa.[6] This in itself does not imply, however, that sickling is a disease specific to the black body—a "racial disease."[7] The distribution of sickling along racial lines in the United States, for instance, could be explained by the Mendelian nature of the disease, and mating patterns produced by the racial politics of American society.[8] Such explanations would not require any allusion to racial biologies. They would, however, force us to interrogate the role of a given social formation in the production and maintenance of human biological attributes. In other words, to explain why sickling continues to be seen as a black-related disease, we need to examine the ideological underpinnings of the research projects and government actions that throughout this century have rendered sickling as a disease of the black body.

The aim of such a project is not to refute the fact that certain diseases are present in some populations and nearly absent in others, but rather to identify what makes it possible to account for such a distribution of disease in terms of race.[9]

Recent incursions of the social sciences into medicine have led to a number of studies on the relation between disease and "race." The medical historian Sander L. Gilman, for example, who has written extensively on pathology and "race," states that "the Jews" as an ideological construct may not have any given diseases, but "jews" may and indeed do.[10] While I agree with Gilman that ethnic and racial categories are ideological constructs, I want to push this notion further than he seems to be willing to do. By introducing the distinction between "the Jews" (an ideological construct) and "jews" ("real" people) and by linking the latter to "real" disease, Gilman implies that race and ethnicity exist inside as well as outside of ideology, and while he denaturalizes one form of "Jewishness," he inadvertently naturalizes another—"jewishness." My position differs from Gilman's in that I believe that "ethnicity" and "race" are always ideological categories; that there is no "reality" disguised by or anterior to these categories.

In examining sickling, a supposedly black-related disease, I hope to show that it is only as discursively defined entities that certain races, ethnic groups, tribes, or communities can be said to constitute the sole locus of a disease. Sickling today is viewed as a black-related disease not simply because the majority of people suffering from the disease are blacks, but because various medical sciences in tandem with anthropology have represented it as a disease of "black people" since the turn of the twentieth century. My point is that medical science and anthropology have used sickling to claim the racial distinctiveness of "blacks" and "whites" and to represent this distinctiveness as the product of a specific genetic structuration—as indisputable fact.[11]

This book then is not about the trait of sickling or the related disease, but rather about how, at specific moments, sickling was established as an object of analysis and a target of intervention, and its identification and treatment became instruments of power.[12] At the very foundation of the book is the observation that, throughout the twentieth century, sickling has emerged and reemerged at the intersection of a variety of medical, genetic, serological, anthropological, personal, and administrative discourses on whiteness, hybridity, tribes, and citizenship. During the 1920s, 1930s, and 1940s, medical researchers used sickling to call into question the racial identity of whites afflicted by the phenomenon. From the 1930s through the 1950s, geneticists and anthropologists seized on the disorder to establish the American Negro (as opposed to the black African living in Africa) as a hybrid and therefore inherently diseased individual. In the 1940s and 1950s, colonial medics and ethnologists saw the occurrence and distribution of sickling in Africa, Southern India, and the Mediterranean area as evidence that tribes were biologically defined entities, and that East Africans, certain Southern Indian populations, and Sicilians and Greeks shared a common racial heritage. Finally, in the 1970s, control and prevention of sickling became the favored corrective measure of the U.S. welfare state eager to make up for its history of discrimination against African Americans, and the emblem of the political goal of full citizenship for African Americans.[13]

This state of affairs, it seems to me, makes the phenomenon of sickling well suited for tracing at least segments of the discursive history of race. Indeed, my aim is to use sickling to outline certain aspects of the genealogy of race. In so doing, I wish to demonstrate, on one hand, that racialist discourses in medicine have been pervasive throughout the twentieth century, and, on the other, that the apparently simple question—What is sickling?—can be answered neither unequivocally nor exhaustively. By showing how discourses on one disease, namely sickling, have historically interfered with and been inflected by discourses on whiteness, hybridity, tribes, citizenship, and race, I hope to illustrate the overall complexity—even messiness—of the discursive field of disease.

Sickling is currently defined in four major discourses: those of clinical medicine, molecular biology, genetics, and biological anthropology.

Clinical medicine accounts for sickling via the typical clinical presentation and medical history of a person with sickle cell anemia: The patient (who can just as well be male as female) is a young adult whose arms and legs are long, skinny, and gangling; her abdomen is short, full, and protruding; her eyes are yellow. She is conspicuously smaller than average for her age and is easily tired. Her first hospitalization, when she was around seven years old, was brought about by severe joint pain, fever, and heart murmurs. At age fourteen, she developed ulcers on both ankles. The ulcers, never fully healed, have turned into a chronic condition. Also around puberty, she started experiencing bouts of excruciating pain, which she still has. Her "crises" typically last up to a week and leave her exhausted and sore all over. During the past decade she has been admitted to the hospital at least once a year and has received about eighty complete blood transfusions.

Molecular biology explains sickling as caused by a mutation in hemoglobin, the protein in red blood cells that carries oxygen to the tissues of the body. The abnormal type of hemoglobin, called hemoglobin S or Hb S (as opposed to normal hemoglobin, Hb A), is sensitive to deficiency of oxygen. When the carrier red blood cells release oxygen to the tissues and the oxygen concentration in those cells is reduced, Hb S stacks in filaments that twist into helical rods in the red blood cells. These rods then cluster into parallel bundles that distort and elongate the cells, causing them to "sickle." From the point of view of molecular biology sickling is the effect of the substitution of one amino acid (valine) for another (glutamic acid) at position 6 on the hemoglobin chain.

Genetics defines sickling as a Mendelian trait, a single recessive point mutation in the individual genome. This mutation leads to a genetically variant but physiologically inefficient abnormality (sickle cell trait) when an individual inherits the gene from a single parent. When the gene is inherited from both parents, the individual has a potentially lethal disease, sickle cell anemia.

Biological anthropology and population genetics consider sickling to be evidence of interaction between the human body and the environment. Pointing to the high incidence of the sickle cell trait in regions around the world where malaria is endemic, anthropologists and geneticists claim that heterozygous individuals (those who inherit a single copy of the gene for sickling) are afforded protection against malaria. (For homozygous individuals—those who inherit two copies of the gene—this advantage is negated by the many deleterious effects of sickle cell anemia.) From the point of view of anthropology and genetics, then, sickling is an instance of natural selection and adaptation in humans.

The discourses on sickling that I have outlined here currently define the phenomenon. None of them tells the full story about sickling, and although they inform and complement each other, they do not provide a definitive account of the disorder when viewed together. My aim in this book, however, is not to assess the validity and completeness of existing discourses on sickling or to identify a heretofore ignored and perhaps "truer" discourse. Rather, it is to bring to light the implied givens of a specified set of medical, genetic, serological, anthropological, administrative, and personal discourse networks that have articulated the study of sickling during the twentieth century.

The term "discourse network" was developed by the German social historian, Friedrich A. Kittler.[14] Informed by the Foucauldian practice of "genealogical" analysis, Kittler uses the strategy of discourse network analysis to delineate the apparatuses of power, knowledge, storage, transmission, reproduction, training, surveillance, and discipline that make it possible to visualize certain objects, rendering them knowable, calculable, manipulable, and, consequently, amenable to administration in the broadest sense of the word. Discourse networks, in Kittler's understanding of the term, are complex and heterogeneous assemblages of inscriptive devices. They give a phenomenon like sickling a particular conceptual shape which, in turn, makes it responsive to specific types of action, whether regulatory, therapeutic, or investigative.

Discourse networks exist in many forms. In the context of sickling, for instance, portraits of sicklers, images of sickle-shaped red blood cells, clinical records of patients with sickle cell anemia, and statistical surveys of sickling rates within given populations are all inscriptive devices, which normalize certain modes of observation and, in the process, constitute sickling as an object of study and intervention.[15]

Discourse networks do not disclose preexisting or hidden truths. Rather, they articulate certain phenomena as natural or unproblematic targets or instruments of specific practices. Thus, visualization, inscription, and articulation, in their contingent facticity and exteriority, are the only irreducible givens of discourse network analysis.

I have pursued sickling as an "effect" that is knowable only through the discourses and practices that at given points in time constitute it and give it meaning. I have not written a general history of sickling, but rather, what Nikolas Rose has termed "a perspectival genealogy of problem spaces, rationalities, authorities and technologies."[16] Thus, I have not presupposed, as others have done, the independent existence of sickling, on the one hand, and its social settings with the theories that come to bear upon it, on the other. Such a rough-and-ready analytic division would imply the existence of a realm of "reality" defined against a realm of reason and power. Such a way of seeing would echo the classic rationalist discourse according to which knowledge moves toward an object that preexists it and from which it extracts its substance.[17] The discourse networks of sickling are passing phenomena that contain no truths that would stop them from undergoing transformations, fading away, or disappearing altogether. They are subject to change because they are inextricably linked to specific historical contexts.

Discourse network analysis is not accepted by those anthropologists, geographers, and sociologists who emphasize subjectivity in their analysis of medicine. To carve out a space for the personal experience of bodily dysfunction and discomfort within the study of medicine, the latter organize their interrogations around the illness/disease dichotomy, where disease signifies the bodily events categorized by biomedicine as specific disorders, and illness refers to the subjective perception and evaluation of, and reaction to these events.[18]

The subjectivist discourse became prominent in contemporary liberal democracies such as the United States and Western European nations during the 1970s owing to the politicization of certain chronic diseases, and the growing awareness of underserved ethnic and other marginalized communities. Rather than putting forth an overall critique of health and medicine within a political economic discourse, this emerging discourse of subjectivity represents the fusion of certain political and medical knowledges, constructing the nation as made up of distinct "cultural" or "ethnic" spaces defined by the diseases that can or can not be found within their boundaries.

The subjectivist discourse has been extensively analyzed by those interested in formulating a critique of medicine's obsession with "dehumanizing" technologies. Thomas Osborne, for instance, sees it as a return to the "sick [wo]man," with [her]/his baggage of a life story, passions, and feelings, a return, that is, to meaningfulness, to the lived experience of sickness that biomedicine has allegedly jettisoned.[19] While it is tempting to be drawn in by the narratives of the sick, especially if one is engaged in socio-anthropological studies of medicine, there are many reasons to resist that temptation. The subjectivist approach to disease takes for granted at least two notions that are at odds with discourse analysis as I have used it here: that subjects exist pre- or extra-discursively, and that indisputably valid truth claims can be made on the basis of personal experience. In subjectivist works, subjects—preferably ethnic or cultural Others—function as primary sources for the construction of meaning.

In this book, I have on a few occasions been concerned with

subjectivities; however, I have considered subjects to be always positioned by discourse networks. Thus, in the context of my analysis, the binarism that contrasts power with agency, for example, has no pertinence. There can be "no single locus of great Refusal, no soul of revolt, source of rebellions, or pure law of the revolutionary,"[20] to borrow Foucault's phrasing. This does not mean that from the point of view of discourse network analysis the notion of agency itself has no analytical pertinence. Agency may be identified, but only as the effect of the various discourses or technologies of inscription that assemble a subject into a particular self. It is discourse networks, practices of subjectification, that produce and systematize certain forms of conduct. Because discourses are not products of conscious acts but rather produce consciousness, they may have different effects at different times. Agency, for instance, can therefore never be specified in advance.[21]

In rejecting the possibility of a pre-discursive subject, discourse network analysis also problematizes the notion of "personal experience" insofar as such experience presupposes the subject. When it comes to putting into question the concept of "personal experience," the physician and anthropologist Arthur Kleinman has staked out nearly unassailable terrain. Kleinman has made a strong and passionate argument for what he calls an "experience-near" ethnography of illness and suffering:

> What categories might an ethnography of experience, in particular one concerned with the study of illness and other forms of suffering, draw upon to resist the tendency toward dehumanizing professional deconstruction, or simply to become more self-consciously reflective about the human core of human experience? It is our opinion that a contextual focus on experience-near categories for ethnography should begin with the defining characteristic of *overbearing practical relevance* in the processes and forms of experience. That is to say, *something is at stake* for all of us in the daily round of happenings and transactions. *Experience* may, on theoretical grounds, be thought of as the intersubjective medium of social transactions in local moral worlds. It is the outcome of cultural categories and social structures interacting with psychophysiological processes such that a mediating world is constituted. Experience is the felt flow of that intersubjective medium.[22] (Italics in original)

Kleinman goes to some length to point out that experience is not a product of human nature. For him, "human conditions— for example, . . . suffering—constrain lived experience."[23] While

I agree with the notion that experience cannot be confined to an origin in consciousness, I am less comfortable with the idea of deriving "meaning," as Kleinman suggests, from an original psychophysiological event such as suffering. In the passage quoted above, Kleinman formulates the cultural and the social as two distinct phenomena interacting with yet another distinct set of events—"psychophysiological processes"—so as to produce a "mediating world" the "felt flow" of which is experience. The problem with this conceptualization of experience from the point of view of discourse network analysis is that it privileges feeling as a vehicle of experience (and knowledge) without specifying the precise nature of feeling. Is it psychological (cultural/social) or physiological (natural) or both? This ambiguity implicitly allows Kleinman to maintain the possibility that an extradiscursive realm exists which ultimately becomes the sine qua non of experience. In other words, Kleinman does not get beyond the classic binary opposition of discourse and reality, and, by extension, that of illness and disease.

What is at stake in not privileging the prefigurative role of experience is the instrumental authority of anthropology. But experience,[24] like conscience or "consciencization" (to use a term proposed by Paul Hirst and Penny Woolley to designate the social production of consciousness), can be located only in culture, and its conditions of possibility must be accounted for through an analysis of the discourse networks that are responsible for its particular systematization at a given time. We simply cannot read it, or its meaning, off of individuals who are thought of as subjects. If we must refuse analytical totalities such as modes of production and society, for instance, then we must reject culture, too, as a register of explanation. For us culture, rather than a system of beliefs and meanings,[25] is that which "unifies a complex of discourses, practices, and institutions as if they expressed a common habitus"[26]—in a word, discourse networks.

In this book no particular discourse has been privileged as a source of some irreducible fact about sickling, not even that of the sufferer—the illness narrative. This is so, because I believe that no phenomenon, not even disease, exists in nature as something that can be known independently or outside of a set of discourses and practices. There are, of course, people who have sickle-shaped red blood cells and people who, in addition to having these cells, throughout their lives, experience repeated bouts of a fixed set of symptoms—some, however infrequent, severe enough to be life threatening and many excruciatingly painful.

However, my main concern has been to examine critically the host of technologies (hospital records, illness narratives, biochemical tests, as well as anthropological, genetic, medical, and political texts) used to record and fix as sickling specific symptoms and a certain blood picture, and to locate the entity thus defined within the black body. Mapping out an ethnography of the sickler,[27] by constructing the meaning of sickling from the perspective of the sick wo/man, or by seeking to document how the disease itself made subjects out of the sicklers, or analyzing how sickling was constructed by the various branches (or paradigms) of medicine—the patient-oriented clinical models of Herrick, Cook, and Meyer as opposed to the laboratory and experimental models of Emmel—would entail reproducing already established models of systematization or normalization of the object. The aim of this book is the reverse, namely to document the specific ways in which the phenomenon has been and still is systematized and normalized.

By not pushing its analysis and theories beyond sickling, this book runs the risk of being read as being "just" about that named disease. While it is possible to demonstrate the contemporaneousness of the concerns identified for sickling in the text by discussing, for example, current works in biomedicine and anthropology linking race to blood pressure (hypertension) and low birth weight, or by examining current discourses on AIDS or taking on the Human Genetic Diversity Project, at the very foundation of discourse network analysis are the notions of temporal and local—that is historical—specificity. Thus, regardless of how closely current concerns in the United States about AIDS as a racial disease track those framing sickling in the very same country during the 1930s, 1940s, and 1950s, they are not identical. Parallels do not entail sameness. What must be avoided, then, is the tendency to use the strategy of comparison to establish claims. Comparative studies all too often favor the broad strokes over the fine print, ultimately undermining, through a certain trivialization, the very argument they are trying to make. All comparison, as I see it, is in the end somewhat superficial and polemical. To claim otherwise would be to enter into the realm of determinism. Fundamentally, the statement that both sickling and AIDS are discursively constructed "racialized" entities says very little.

Yet this book has something to convey beyond what it says about sickling. My hope is that it will make a case for discourse network analysis as a strategy that, when carefully applied, has the potential to examine and problematize the political pertinence and signifying cultural expressions of such phenomena as sickling, AIDS, and the Human Genetic Diversity Project.

Discourse network analysis does not claim to be exhaustive and definitive. It simply lays bare the structuration of power at a given point in space and time. At the foundation of the strategy is the notion that while the mechanisms of power can be rendered less effective by being exposed, their exposure will eventually be followed by the emergence of new and different mechanisms of power. Indeed, this inherent transformability of power is the condition of possibility of change—sometimes for the better, often, unfortunately, for the worse.[28]

Chapter 1
Interrogating Bodies

When Is a Caucasian Not a Caucasian?

Our white, Optic white . . . Our white is so white you can paint a chunka coal and you'd have to crack it open with a sledge hammer to prove it wasn't white clear through!
—Ralph Ellison, *Invisible Man* (1947)

The racial specificity [of sickle cell anemia] is unique. If found to hold true, this would indicate that the primary basis for the disease must be laid in conditions far removed from any possible accident of the environment. . . . [W]e must assume that the disease depends primarily on some fundamental racial peculiarity of the blood forming tissues.
—G. S. Graham, "A Case of Sickle Cell Anemia with Necropsy" (1924)

Medical historian David McBride's account of the response of the medical community and the national health agencies in the United States to the tuberculosis epidemic, which ravaged the African American community in the first half of the twentieth century, also describes the racialist context in which early research on sickling took place.[1] McBride shows that the dominant medical paradigm until World War I was what he calls "sociomedical racialism," whereas the period after World War I was characterized by the rise of a new medical order which he labels "scientific epidemiology."[2] McBride defines sociomedical racialism as based on the notion that disease and other "abnormalities" can best be accounted for in terms of anatomical—that is to say inherited "racial" —features. A disproportionate number of African Americans died from tuberculosis (the African American mortality rate was two to four times higher than that of white Americans) because African Americans were either "natural" carriers of or "naturally" susceptible to that disease: "In the first two decades of the century phenotypical racialism had consumed the medical and social welfare communities' perceptions and responses to the health problems of black Americans. Brown skin and African features had been an icon for susceptibility to bodily disease."[3] McBride defines "scientific epidemiology," in contrast, as considering disease to be a function not only of anatomy or "racial" inheritance but also of the environment: "[The] key idea was that, while it may be theoretically possible to delineate races using certain phenotypical or genotypical criteria, black and white Americans had essentially similar inborn immunity and susceptibility to disease. . . . Race, then, was only one index to possible disease susceptibility."[4]

McBride presents sociomedical racialism and scientific epidemiology as two radically distinct perspectives, but I would argue that they are continuous. They both actively (if not equally aggressively) promote the notion of racial peculiarity or racial difference. Whereas sociomedical racialism relies on early anthropological phenotypical and genotypical criteria for race and poses the "black body" as inherently diseased, scientific epidemiology attributes the "unfitness" of the black body to environmental factors. Yet because these reworkings of causation in favor of history and the environment do not call into question the phenotypical and genotypical determination of "race," scientific epidemiology is not qualitatively different from sociomedical racialism. Both approaches incorporate the assumption of the anatomic (inherited racial) specificity of blacks.

From the very beginning, the study of the clinical picture and the cell geometry of sickling also produced a racialist reading of the disease.[5] In 1922, for instance, the physician Verne Mason reporting only the fourth case of sickling in the U.S., suggested that "it is of particular interest that up to the present the malady has been seen only in the negro, and, so far as could be ascertained, it is the only disease peculiar to that race."[6] Mason's comment directs us not just to an arithmetic of reported cases of sickling but to the notion of "racially specific" diseases. By taking Mason's conclusion into account, we can assess what made possible the racialization of sickling: medical science's embrace of the anthropological notion of "racial" specificity and difference.

When the hereditary nature of the disease was characterized in the early 1920s,[7] the notion of inheritability was understood exclusively in racial terms, as the epigraph from G. S. Graham indicates. Borrowing a phrase from the art historian Griselda Pollock, one might say that heredity and race were seen as "historical simultaneities and mutually inflecting."[8]

The concept of race also came to play an important role in the classification of the anemias. In an influential paper entitled "Likenesses and Contrasts in the Hemolytic Anemias of Childhood," the physician T. B. Cooley distinguished three types of anemias —"congenital hemolytic icterus," "von Kaksch's ('erythroblastic') anemia," and "sickle cell anemia," all of which he saw as particular articulations of a single anemia—"hemolytic jaundice."[9] Cooley's organization of the anemias is pertinent here because, as we shall see below, it involves not only the parameters of blood cell geometry and heredity, but also (and prominently so) that of race:

> Sickle cell anemia is distinctly racial and possibly originally limited to a small section of the negro race. The erythroblastic anemia is so conspicuously more common in the Mediterranean races as to seem almost peculiar to them; while hemolytic jaundice, though more wide spread than the other two, tends decidedly to be more frequent in certain regions and among certain people, and to appear only sporadically elsewhere. In other words, in all three the diathesis [constitutional predisposition] seems distinctly a matter of family or race. . . . These diseases might be thought of as three types of hemolytic jaundice, each depending on a congenital diathesis, and each strikingly limited to familial or racial groups.[10]

What Cooley belabors above is first the usefulness of heredity and race in sorting the anemias. But it is also the usefulness of the anemias in classifying populations or races. For implied in Cooley's statement is the idea that populations and "races" can be categorized in terms of their differential rates of any given anemia. In proposing a classification of the anemias in terms of blood cell geometry *and* race, Cooley constituted the various anemias as (more or less) unequivocal expressions of "racial" specificity. After Cooley, it was no longer the distinctiveness of the specific anemias that was at stake in the classification of these pathologies but rather the racial identity of the individual diagnosed with a given anemia.

Two years after Mason established a link between race and sickling based on only four cases (his own and three previously reported ones), V. P. Sydenstricker reached the same conclusion through an entirely new strategy favoring a very different method. Rather than relying exclusively on full-blown cases, Sydenstricker drew upon the idea of "latent" or, as Victor Emmel termed them, "potential" cases of sickling.[11] Whereas the old strategy of case finding relied upon the patient/doctor interaction (where the sick person came to the clinic with specific complaints which the doctor then interrogated and assigned meaning), the new strategy employed by Sydenstricker produced cases by analyzing blood samples in the laboratory. By privileging the laboratory over the clinic as a site of production of "valid" medical knowledge, Sydenstricker came to consider as "patients" people who did not feel ill or who—if they were sick—did not necessarily have sickle cell anemia.[12] Consider this summary of Sydenstricker's report: "The blood of more than 300 white patients has been examined by us with special reference to 'latent sickling,' and in no case has anything resembling it been seen. In a similar number of negroes, it was found thirteen times, exclusively of its occurrence in the families in the cases reported."[13]

Here the clinical gaze shifts from the individual patient, his or her complaints and biography (name, age, race, gender, occupation, marital status, and geographical location), to racial populations. Stating that "there is strong [statistical] evidence that [sickling] occurs only in the negro race or in persons of mixed blood," Sydenstricker became the first medical scientist to represent sickling as *statistically* linked to race.[14] Sydenstricker's work led to a series of statistical studies on the blood of hospitalized patients designed to ascertain whether sickling was indeed "confined" to the "black body," as reported. All these studies used anonymous blood samples drawn from hundreds of hospitalized patients identified only by race. T. B. Cooley and P. Lee examined the blood of 400 black hospital patients in Detroit and found 30 cases (7.5 percent) of sickling.[15] G. S. Graham and S. H. McCarty, working in Birmingham, Alabama, examined the blood of 608 "colored" patients from the medical, surgical, and obstetrical wards and found 44 instances of sickling (7.2 percent).[16] H. W. Josephs, in his study of 250 "colored" patients in Baltimore, found 16 cases of sickling (6.4 percent).[17] And K. Miyamoto and J. G. Korb from St. Louis, Missouri, examined the blood of 100 white patients and found no cases of sickling.[18] These findings all seemed to indicate that sickling was indeed linked to race: a particular cell geometry (the sickle-shaped cell) could be seen as a marker of "racial" specificity (blackness).

Statistical analyses and surveys played an important role in establishing sickling as a black-related disease. Yet, far from locating an objective truth about the relationship between sickling and race, the statistical approach reproduced the dominant ideology and social organization of the period. Reflecting the view of their society, Sydenstricker and his colleagues took for granted—and organized their research around—a distinction between black and white bodies. They localized sickling in already established spaces between black and white bodies without ever calling into question the ideological nature or foundation of these spaces.

All those diagnosed by Sydenstricker and his colleagues as having sickling in their blood were said to be "colored" or "black." As a consequence of this equation of sickling with nonwhite people, a diagnosis of sickling in an individual who was reported to be white immediately raised questions about the accuracy of the sickling test, as well as about the true racial identity of the diagnosed individual. This not only because early epidemiological studies failed to find sickling among whites, but also because medicine employed the black body and others who came in contact with it as exemplary markers of sickling. What was ultimately at stake in the inquisition of the "white" bodies in which sickling was found was not sickling (the clinical entity) but the racial purity (the degree of nonblackness) of these bodies.

*   *   *

In 1925 V. Castana, a clinician from Italy, set in motion a heated debate about the relationship between race and sickling among clinicians within the United States. Castana reported finding what he called "semilunar gigantocyte cells" in a "white" Italian child. Castana concluded that "there is not a well defined anemia with semi-circular cells but different blood diseases, with gigantic cell rings, semi-circular, sickle- and long-shaped cells."[19] Over the next two decades, the literature on sickling in individuals who could not easily (that is, visually) be fixed as "black" continued to develop. By 1943, the New York physician Louis Greenwald and his colleagues were able to review seventeen published reports on the phenomenon.

The early reports included several cases of nonblack patients. In 1926, R. G. Archibald, a physician working in the Sudan at the time, reported a case of sickling in a ten-year-old Sudanese boy, who was of Arab ancestry.[20] Almost immediately after Archibald's report, J. S. Lawrence and W. B. Stewart, two American physicians, independently reported finding sickling in two white families. Passages from these two cases show what was at stake. Lawrence's case involved

a woman of Spanish and Scotch-Irish descent who came to the hospital complaining of disability in walking. . . . Special attention was paid to the question of racial admixture of negro blood in the family but no evidence could be obtained. On the maternal side, the great-great-grandmother came from Spain and the great-great-grandfather from France. On the paternal side, the ancestry was Scotch-Irish, and the great-grandparents are thought to have settled in Virginia. . . . There must be some caution in calling this sickle cell anemia because no evidence of negro blood could be found.[21]

Stewart's case was as follows:

F. D., aged 6 years, was seen first on June 24, 1921, at the age of 5 months . . . for acute gastroenteritis. . . . The child was not seen again until March 8, 1925, at the age of 4 years, when he was admitted . . . with acute pain in the upper part of the abdomen, swollen, tender ankle and fever. . . . On April 23, 1926, another attack of abdominal pain and another crop of lesions of the skin appeared, together with a patch of pneumonia in the lower lobe of the left lung. Then for the first time sickle cells were sought and found in the blood of the patient. Discovery of the sickle cells led to a closer examination of the family. The patient had the features of an octoroon: fair skin, light kinky hair, thick lips and slightly flattened nose. The father . . . was a healthy white man without negro characteristics, and without sickle cells in his blood. The mother was also white, but had the dark skin and features of a Cuban. She had always been weak and nervous, and smears of her blood showed a small proportion of sickle cells. There were four other children; none of them had any decidedly negroid features, although the youngest had a few sickle cells in smears of her blood. Neither parent knew of the existence of any negro forbears; the father's maternal grandparents were English and Jewish, and the mother's maternal grandparents were Cuban. The family lived in a district bordering on the colored section, but by their neighbors they were classed among the whites. . . . If this should be an instance of sickle cell anemia in a white person, it would be the first on record. However, the facial characteristics of the patient indicated a mixture of colored with white blood at some time in the past, for which the Cuban ancestry affords distinct opportunity. The crossing of races among certain elements of the Cubans has been notorious. But in the last three generations of this family, which can be traced with certainty, there have not been any negroes.[22]

Key phrases in these passages from Lawrence and Stewart are "racial admixture," "negro blood," "negro characteristics," "negroid features," "mixture of colored with white blood," and "a crossing of the races." Borrowed from traditional physical anthropology, these terms all imply the notion of an inherent racial difference between black and white bodies. This notion, in turn, permits the concepts of "racial" purity and impurity, which are challenged by the findings of sickling, a supposedly black-related disease in whites (or nonblacks).

Lawrence and Stewart faced the same problem: Given the received anthropological construction of "racial" identity, which relied on visible characteristics of the individual and which had so successfully produced the distinction between white and black bodies, making the blood the ultimate locus of this "racial" distinctiveness, how could one make sense of one's findings of sickle-shaped blood cells — markers of blackness — in an apparently white patient?

The passage from Stewart contains two competing constructions of racial identity. Stewart states that "by their neighbors they [his patient and his family] were classed as whites." He does not, however, take into account this local (social) construction of race, which seriously jeopardizes the notion of sickling as a black-related disease. Instead, he relies heavily (exclusively) on the criteria for "race" put forward by the medical and anthropological literature of the time: physiognomy (what does the patient look like?) and genealogy (who are his or her ancestors and where did they come from?). In so doing, Stewart effectively raises questions about the authenticity of his case. The facial characteristics of the patient are said to indicate an "admixture with negro blood in the past"; and his Cuban ancestry is seen as an indication of racial impurity. Here Stewart is obviously drawing upon the commonly accepted perception of Cuba (at the time) as a "notorious" (Rosenfeld and Pincus call it "violent") "racial melting pot."[23] Like other places in the Americas with a sizable African population, Cuba was seen as affording "distinct opportunity" for "cross-breeding" because its legal statutes (supposedly), unlike those in the United States, did not regulate the interaction between blacks and whites.[24]

In 1929, Cooley and Lee, now well respected in the field of sickling, published a report on sickling in whites that was the first such case widely accepted as authentic. The patients, all members of a Greek-American family, were acknowledged to be incontestably "racially pure whites." But considering how controversial the issue of linking sickling with the racial identity of people who "looked" white—optic whites—was at the time, what provided scientific legitimation for Cooley and Lee? How did they prove that they saw cells that were truly sickle-shaped and patients who were indeed "racially pure whites"? The controversy centered not only around the racial physiognomy of the subjects, but also around the locality in which they were born and lived (geography) and their family tree (genealogy). Cooley and Lee pieced together narratives of their patients' family histories, providing information about their nationality, their place of birth and that of their relatives (siblings, parents, and grandparents), the length of time that their family had lived in a given region, the racial composition of the population of that region, the contacts that this population had had with "Negroes," and reports of similar illnesses in other people from the region. They enclosed photos of their patients, along with photomicrographs of fresh, stained blood film depicting the sickle-shaped cells to provide visual proof for their claims.

Cooley and Lee's strategy for establishing the racial identity of their subjects does not appear to be significantly different from Stewart's. So what allowed Cooley and Lee to conclude that "these are the first observations of definite sickle cell anemia in subjects regarding whom *no reasonable suspicion* can be raised of an admixture of negro blood" (emphasis added)? [25] And why did the medical establishment accept this conclusion? Mainly because Cooley and Lee's subjects came to the United States from Greece—from "Byregos, a small village in the Peloponnesus near Olympia where their families had long been residents and where negroes are said to be unknown"—as opposed to Stewart's patient, who was of Cuban descent. Since Greece was seen as the cradle of Western culture, Greeks were considered prototypically white.[26]

In 1930, George S. Graham and Sarah H. McCarty subjected all the published sickling cases involving "whites" to a critical review. They arrived at the following conclusion:

> Our current knowledge of the disease has been developed in this country. Little attention has been accorded in Europe although reviews of the American work have appeared in France and Germany. A number of continental writers have however, described crescentric erythrocytes in a varied list of diseases, particularly in malaria. Castana in Italy (dealing presumably with white patients) has recently reported cases of anemia with crescentric erythrocytes in the blood smear. The latter identifies them definitely with the cells reported in sickle cell anemia and questions the existence of a separate complex such as has been claimed by writers in this country. Castana offers no picture and his description is difficult of interpretation, but there is considerable doubt whether he or other continental writers have dealt with the true meniscocyte [sickling]. Lawrence similarly, has reported the occurrence of sickle cells in both healthy and ill white and colored individuals. Again, there is doubt whether he dealt actually with the cell under discussion. The only undoubted case that we have found reported from abroad is that of Archibald. The case is of special interest as bearing upon the question of racial specificity.[27]

For Graham and McCarty, the mere presence of the sickling erythrocytes in the blood was sufficient proof that the patient had sickling only in cases involving undisputedly "black" individuals. In all other cases, diagnosing sickling was problematic. There was always, as Graham and McCarty put it, "considerable doubt" as to whether the physician assigning the diagnosis had correctly identified the cells he was dealing with. As increasing numbers of cases of sickling in "whites" were reported, physicians were faced with the dilemma of either rejecting these cases on the grounds that the diagnosed individuals were not truly "white" or that the cells found in their blood were not authentic sickle-shaped cells, or creating a space within which sickling in whites would cease to be problematic. They chose the latter solution and refined existing strategies to determine who was and who was not "racially pure white," without accepting the position that sickling could be found in "whites."

It was no simple matter to determine racial identity. Once thought to be situated at the (visible) surface of the body, race had to be moved to a deeper and hidden level (that of the cell) and into space and time (geography and history). The visible surface of the body had ceased to convey unequivocally whether a person was black or white, as physiognomy, the unquestionable index for race, began to lose its coherence.

The practice of revealing "black" ancestry in "apparently [pure] white" people with sickling eventually became commonplace. Samuel Rosenfeld and Joseph B. Pincus—a pathologist and pediatrician, respectively, working in New York—systematically refute the claim to "whiteness" in previously identified sickling cases:

From the ethnological view-point there is great interest in the question as to whether sickle cells ever occur in white persons in whom there is no suspicion of admixture of negro blood. In the literature there is much confusion on this point, which is chiefly one to mistaking other deformities of the red blood cells for sickling or to a strong suspicion of admixture of negro blood in cases with true sickling. . . . The first report of sickle-cell anemia in a white person is that of Castana. . . . In eliminating this case there are several points to be considered. In the first place, there are no illustrations. Second, there is no mention of the behavior of the patient's red cells in sealed preparations, an essential test in determining sickling. Third, and most important, . . . the semi-lunar or sickle-like gigantocytes [described by Castana] . . . represent degenerate erythrocytes and are not true sickle cells. . . . [The] second case . . . was reported by Archibald. This was a typical case of sickle-cell anemia, illustrated by convincing photographs, in an Arab boy, . . . a native of the Sudan. The parents were both Arabs. Nothing is stated of the possible presence of negro blood in the family tree, nor is any mention made regarding the appearance of the features of the patient or of his parents. Since the residence of the patient is in a region where the inhabitants are predominantly negro and where interbreeding is notoriously common, the probability of an admixture of negro blood in this case is very strong. The third case . . . was in an apparently white child with facial characteristics of a negro—features of an octaroon, kinky hair, thick lips, and a flattened nose. The father was a healthy white man. . . . The mother, although considered a white person by her neighbors, had a dark skin and the features of a Cuban, and was of Cuban descent. It is well known that Cuba is a violent melting pot, with the negro the predominant type. . . . In 1929 Cooley and Lee reported [a case of sickling in] a white child of Greek descent. The description of the case and the photographs of the blood are convincing. Sights and Simon described a case [of] a white native American of Scotch-Irish parentage. The absence of a racial and geographical study of other members of the patient's family to exclude the possible admixture of negro blood decreases considerably the value of this case from an ethnologic viewpoint.[28]

Rosenfeld and Pincus then describe what for them is the "third [case of sickling] . . . in a white person where no evidence of admixture of negro blood can be discovered":

A boy, aged 9 years, was admitted [with the] complaint of intermittent attacks of abdominal pain for the past 5 years. The father . . . was born in the town of Reggio, Calabria, which is in southern Italy, where his family lived for generations and where negroes are unknown. A brother of his, whose blood shows no sickle cells, is certain that his parents and grandparents had no negro features. The mother of the patient, whose blood shows sickle cells . . . was born in the United States, where she has lived her entire life. She has a muddy complexion, but she has no features suggestive of the negro. She has 2 children, of whom 1 is the patient. The other child, aged 12 years, has no features suggestive of the negro and has sickle cells in her blood. The mother has 3 sisters and several brothers, none of whom shows anything suggestive of the colored race. The mother's parents and her forbears for generations were born and lived in Casabona, a town in Calabria, Italy. Here there has always been a strict social custom against intermarriage with other races. Negroes are unknown in this region; and in this connection it is interesting to note that the grandmother of the patient never saw a negro until she came to the United States at the age of about 25. The sickling trait has been definitely found in three generations of the family; and in at least five generations it is known that the members have been of the white race.[29]

Notwithstanding the above scrutiny, Rosenfeld and Pincus do not unconditionally accept the authenticity of the case:

The possibility cannot be absolutely ruled out that in a previous remote generation, there might have been a negro ancestor with sickle cells in the blood and that the sickling trait . . . might have been handed down thereby to white descendants with no external trace of any of the negro features. This possibility must receive serious consideration, for the weight of evidence seems to indicate the negro origin of sickling. . . .

It is to be expected that in the future more cases of sickle-cell anemia in white persons will be discovered. First, since attention has been called to the occurrence of the sickling trait in the white race. . . . Second, since it is known that the sickling trait is a dominant character in its hereditary transmission, and since interbreeding between the colored and the white races is more or less constantly taking place in many regions, including this country, we may in future generations expect the presence of this peculiar blood trait in an increasing number of apparently white descendants. Because of the tendency to deny such descent by those who are free of all negro features, no history will be obtained of such racial origin in affected individuals, thereby increasing the number of apparently pure white cases of sickle-cell anemia.[30]

Rosenfeld and Pincus try to come to terms with the findings of sickling in whites by insisting on the existence of the "apparently pure white" individual. This concept, which is constantly evoked in the literature on sickle cell anemia, is akin to that of the mulatto who passes as "white" which was a fixture in literature of the time as well as in the social sciences. As the historian Paul R. Spickard observes, "From the 1920s to the 1940s, no book on black people or race-relations was complete without a section on passing."[31]

Foucault has said that it is difficult to determine who has power, but very easy to know who does not. One could say the same about whiteness. There are few ways of assessing who is truly white but many ways of determining who is not. The concept of the "apparently white" person is, in a general way, yet another means of raising doubts about certain people's identification as white. In the context of sickling, it was a means of maintaining the status of this phenomenon as a "black-related disease."

*   *   *

Physiognomy alone could no longer be entrusted to confirm racial identity, as the growing number of sickling cases in apparently white people indicated, and genealogy—the scrutiny of a patient's ancestry for the purpose of exposing an "alien" (that is to say black) ancestor—became increasingly important as a means of ruling out "pure whiteness." But the genealogical method could not arrive at a cutoff point that was not arbitrary and beyond which one could be certain of a person's racial identity. Having ruled out black ancestry in their subjects for three and five generations, respectively, Stewart as well as Rosenfeld and Pincus were still unable to accept their subjects' claim to be "racially pure whites."

As neither physiognomy nor genealogy could ever definitively prove whether racial admixture had taken place, sickling researchers were faced with the dilemma: either recognize sickling as a phenomenon that also occurred in the white body, or find new strategies for showing that cross-breeding had indeed occurred (thereby perpetuating the idea of distinct racial stocks and vindicating the status of the sickling erythrocytes as racial markers).

Recognizing sickling as a fact of the white body would entail acknowledging that sickling was not a valid marker of racial difference. It would also call into question the very notion of "racial" difference and such commonly accepted signs of this particular form of difference (established by nineteenth-century physical anthropologists) as hair texture and color, eye color, head shape, and stature. The sickling researchers chose to maintain the status of sickling as a "black-related" disease by introducing the elements of history and geography in their assessment of "racial" purity and difference and by constructing the category of the "apparently white" individual.

A closer scrutiny of specific groups of whites in which high numbers of sickling were found revealed that the vast majority were of Southern European origin. The physician Louis Greenwald and his colleagues speak directly to this point:

It seems more than a coincidence that these, and all the patients to be reported, are of South Italian stock. The not infrequent occurrence of the sickle cell trait in Puerto Ricans and Mexicans is understandable, because of the high incidence of crossbreeding with the negro race. In tracing the derivation of those patients whose family history admits of no such mixture, one is struck by the high proportion with Mediterranean background.[32]

Greenwald and his colleagues do not hesitate to call upon the "admixture" theory to account for sickling in "non-black" European populations. This theory proves to be "unproblematic" when accounting for sickling in Puerto Ricans and Mexicans because, according to Greenwald and his coauthors, these people are known to have "a high incidence of crossbreeding with the negro race." In other words, the presence of difference ("impurity") in the Other (Puerto Ricans, Mexicans, and so forth) is seen as "natural," the presumption being that the Other, in any case, is a whirlpool of "impurity" that contaminates everything with which it comes into contact.

When it comes to white individuals of Mediterranean background, however, the theory seems less applicable because it is taken for granted that these individuals are racially "pure." If sickling is incontestably and exclusively linked to the black body, how can its appearance in white Mediterraneans be understood? Greenwald et al. suggest that

It is a moot question, whether, as some students of the disease predicate, a negro strain was introduced during the migrations and wars of ancient or even earlier times, or whether the sickle cell trait need not carry any connotation of negro heritage. The subject has more than ethnologic or historic interest, for it may be a clue to the diagnosis and understanding of a hitherto bizarre and unrecognized group of hemolytic anemias.[33]

They claim that the paradox of sickling in "whites" would be resolved if a "negro strain" could be identified in the Mediterranean
population. The introduction of such a strain would preferably
have to be an event of the remote past. Individual genealogy is
thus subjugated to a collective genealogy (the overall history of
the people, in particular its migrations and wars) when it comes to
assessing the racial purity of those whites diagnosed with sickling.
The following observation from the physician M. A. Ogden is exemplary of this historicizing strategy:

> The problem of whether this condition is confined to the Negro race or
> may occur in members of white and yellow races without admixture of
> Negro blood is not yet satisfactorily solved. However, I have a right to my
> strong conviction that the sickling trait is a condition found in the Negro
> race only [and] that all cases in which members of white families have such
> a trait . . . an admixture of Negro blood . . . has taken place. . . . It can be
> concluded that all white persons with sickle cell anemia . . . have been per-
> sons of Mediterranean origin (Greeks, Italians, Sicilians and Spaniards),
> with the exception of one American family. . . . Every living person, if one
> goes back twenty-four generations, had in the early thirteenth century
> 16,713,216 ancestors . . . If one consider this fact, it becomes obvious that
> *it is practically impossible to exclude with any degree of certainty the existence of an
> admixture of Negro blood in some members of the white race.* Hannibal's invasion
> of Spain and Italy, the Moorish occupation of southern Spain, slave trade
> with Africa, . . . *brought the Negro into close contact with whites.*[34] (Empha-
> sis added)

A similar point was made earlier by F. Clarke, another clinician,
who saw as significant not only the history of the population, but
also its geographical location:

> I am reliably informed that there is more or less intermarriage between
> the Sicilians and the Greek. . . . In view of the early history of Sicily,
> Italy, and Greece, and their *geographical proximity to Africa,* it would seem
> possible if not probable that admixture of negro blood [has occurred] in
> both these races. Sicily was originally a province of Carthage, Africa, and
> was inhabited by Greeks, Italians and Africans. It follows then that the
> possible admixture of negro blood is not entirely eliminated in the cases
> thus reported as occurring in the white race.[35] (Emphasis added)

The argument of Greenwald et al., as well as that of Ogden and
Clarke, is that even if the Mediterranean people diagnosed with
sickling bear no external signs of difference (of being nonwhite)

and thus cannot immediately be categorized as having hybridized with blacks (as mulattos), their blood has *probably* been contaminated through contact with Africans—a contact said to have been brought about by historical and geographical circumstances (invasion, wars, occupation, and "proximity to Africa").

On the one hand, the occurrence of sickling in white non-European individuals (Mexicans, Puerto Ricans) is linked to association with black people in the present or recent past. In such a view, a scrutiny of the individual genealogy is needed to document miscegenation. On the other hand, sickling in white Europeans (Italians, Greeks, and others) is presented as a result of association with blacks in the remote past. In this case there is, therefore, a need to map not only the genealogy of a single individual but that of a people—its history of exposure to peoples of African descent through migration, wars, and invasions. Here it is seen as important, then, that the "white" Europeans in question are *Southern* Europeans existing in a space defined by its geographical proximity to Africa.

The creation of an additional criterion for whiteness (not to be afflicted by sickling) problematized the racial identity of Southern Europeans with seemingly unquestionable "white" credentials. More precisely, it made possible the representation of Southern Europeans as racially distinct from other assimilated whites. The disorder came to be seen as "writing in blood" a long history of cultural (migration, war and conquest) and biogenetic (admixture) exchange between certain European Mediterranean regions and Africa.

The representation of Southern Europeans as, in Ellison's words, "not white clear through," was made possible by the reemergence of a virulent racialist discourse during the 1920s—the period when many sickling researchers received their training. John Higham, a historian of the early twentieth century, refers to the time as the "tribal twenties."[36] The success of *The Passing of the Great Race* by Madison Grant and *The Rising Tide of Color Against White World Supremacy* by his disciple Lothrop Stoddard attests to the legitimacy and pervasiveness of racialism at the time. *The Passing of the Great Race* was well received by such major publications as the *New York Times* and the *Saturday Evening Post*. It identified and popularized a three-tiered hierarchical structure within the white population: Nordics, Alpines, and Mediterraneans. The "American people"

(Anglo-Saxon Americans—blacks and other people of color were not considered to belong to this category) was, Grant preached, to keep from engaging in racial mixing with the Alpines and Mediterraneans to stave off the destructive process of "mongrelization." Kenneth Roberts, Grant's protegé, formulated this view even more succinctly. In "Why Europe Leaves Home" published by the *Saturday Evening Post*, he warned that the continuing influx of Alpine, Mediterranean, and Semitic immigrants would overrun the Nordic population and produce "a hybrid race of people as worthless and futile as the good-for-nothing mongrels of Central America and Southeastern Europe."[37]

It is beside the point here to argue that many Southern Europeans were "misdiagnosed" with sickling—as opposed to Cooley's anemia (thalassemia), supposedly the right diagnosis—because of the similarity between sickling and thalassemia. Such an apology would support a racialist project that has yet to reach a closure. The case of the "misdiagnosed" Southern Europeans is fascinating because it reflects the fact that their physicians had appropriated a discourse about them that, by the 1930s and 1940s, appeared to have ceased to inform social relations among whites.

What we see (once again) is a rearrangement of the floating lines of demarcation of the white body rather than an acceptance of the occurrence of sickling in whites. New criteria are being added to an already extensive list used to exclude certain bodies from the status of whiteness.

The racial identity of a body is, in this historical-geographic context, not a merely biological matter to be resolved at the level of the individual but also, in a subtle way, a function of the "contamination" to which an entire social body (a population) could plausibly have been exposed through contacts with social bodies different from itself. In the case of the Mediterranean population, "contamination" is deemed likely to have taken place due to remote historical circumstances and because of the geographical proximity of the Mediterranean and the African continents. The bodies of the Southern European populations (which in other contexts would be categorized as white) were turned into borderline cases as geographical and historical criteria were introduced to assess racial identity.

*   *   *

In the first half of the twentieth century, sickling played an important role in substantiating the notion of the racial distinctiveness of "white" and "black" bodies and, paradoxically, in destabilizing the very notion of whiteness: Sometimes a Caucasian is not a Caucasian. As authorized experts on "racial" difference, physicians who worked on sickling had to invent the notion of the "apparently white" individual in order not to undermine the legitimacy of their project. It is ironic that this destabilization of whiteness would take place in the work of physicians who thought of themselves as attending to the science or truth of the black body and its signs.

Chapter 2
An "Anthropathology" of the "American Negro," 1940–1952

Medical historians of nineteenth- and early twentieth-century North American racial history have given much attention to the early discursive fusion of anthropology and medicine which would eventually lead to the "pathologization" of the "American Negro."[1] John S. Haller, for example, has pointed out how, beginning in the mid-nineteenth century, medicinal researchers (in particular Southern physicians with a hereditarian or vitalist bend) drew upon anthropological information about race to evaluate census reports, extensive statistics compiled by the Army on the health of recruits, and actuarial information from insurance companies in order to show that the American Negro was well on the way to extinction. Using the guise of social Darwinism, Haller argues, these physicians endorsed the idea of the survival of the fittest, whether individuals or aggregates of individuals such as "races," and presented the American Negro as less than fit.[2]

However, while much of the original theoretical framework for the formation of the American Negro as an object of knowledge was supplied by anthropology, medicine remained the dominant force in this endeavor until the 1920s. This situation was explicitly recognized in 1926 when the National Research Council formed the Committee on the Negro to promote anthropological and psychological research in this area. Reflecting on the state of knowledge regarding the Negro, the physical anthropologist Ales Hrdlicka, a member of the committee, observed that the literature in general was "scattered" and its "incompleteness" made it of questionable importance. "[But] among the earliest observations on the American negro of more or less scientific nature," he proclaimed, "are those of some of the medical men who were brought into a closer contact with the race."[3]

Thus, as anthropology began to focus on the Negro in particular, rather than on race in general, it was tackling a subject on which most of the existing information had been gathered by physicians or investigators with a medical orientation. The subject matter was structured by concepts, concerns, and practices that were at the time specific to medical science, namely, normality, pathology, race mixture, degeneracy, and—by practical extension—segregation and surveillance. Many early-twentieth-century "medical men" saw the Negro as becoming extinct, not because of the inherent "unfitness" of the race as nineteenth-century "medical men" would have it, but because of admixture of "white" blood (the notion of the "whitening" or "bleaching" of the Negro was central to their discourse).[4] It is not surprising then that the emerging anthropological discourse on the Negro was organized around the concept of hybridity and aimed to examine the socio-medical consequences of such a practice for the overall Negro population.[5] Although the exponents for the new medico-anthropological discourse did not uncritically hark back to the brutal work of nineteenth-century Darwinian physicians[6]—who invoked anthropological science to establish a link between disease and racial and hereditary biology, in order to make visible how nature removes the unfit from the social body through natural selection—they did take for granted that race is a biological and hereditary feature whose role in disease can be ascertained, or, inversely, that *a* race is partially defined by its members' susceptibility to certain diseases.[7]

One of the representatives of the new medico-anthropological discourse, Julian H. Lewis, a physician who eventually became director of research at Providence Hospital, Chicago, later explicitly outlined and named the anthropathological project, the assessment of which is at the core of this chapter. Lewis showed an early interest in serological anthropology, especially in the "biochemical index of race" developed by the Polish serologists Ludwik and Hanna Hirszfeld.[8] In 1922, Lewis and Deborah L. Henderson carried out the first survey of blood types among American Negroes with the aim of comparing the biochemical index of race (as expressed in terms of blood grouping) for American Negroes with that proposed by the Hirszfelds for African Negroes.[9] The purpose here was not yet to link race and disease, but simply to identify—or define—the Negro in biochemical terms. However, twenty-six years later, in 1948, in a lecture to the Fellows of the Institute of Medicine of Chicago, Lewis proposed a research program that effectively added disease to an already long list of biological indices of race:

[I]t is to be expected that the various human groups, loosely called "races," will exhibit differences in the kind of diseases that affect them and in the way they react to these diseases. Anthropological descriptions of a group of people are incomplete if they do not also include a statement as to behavior to disease, because this trait is as much a characteristic of them as is the color of the eyes or stature. Nor can the evolutionary development be described and explained without taking into account the effect of disease.[10]

Whereas traditional anthropological surveys of such features as "the color of the eyes or stature" aimed to map phenotypical variations among races, Lewis's concern was to map something that could not immediately be visualized but nevertheless was part of their "racial essence," namely their susceptibility to disease.

In his lecture in 1948, Lewis stressed the significance of medical scientists and anthropologists working in tandem on the issues of race and disease. He told the Fellows, "Indeed, there is considerable information in anthropological literature that is of much importance to medicine and in turn anthropologists make free use of knowledge developed by physicians." As an example of this mutual benefit Lewis pointed to the study of blood groups: "Discovered by medical scientists and used as a basis of successful blood transfusion, blood grouping has been extensively used by anthropologists to classify races and to demonstrate racial origins." He outlined how doctors could obtain crucial information about the etiology of disease by using anthropological insights concerning race and concluded that "the study of the comparative behavior of disease among races deserves a special term for its designation." He suggested the word "anthropathology" for that purpose.[11]

According to Lewis, the Negro would be particularly well suited for anthropathological studies:

The literature concerning him is extensive, the environmental and biologic characteristics of Negroes and Caucasians show marked contrasts in many relations, and a knowledge of the behavior of disease among Negroes has much practical value. Such a study affords a possibility of evaluating many factors that may influence disease. Groups of American Negroes are available who live or have lived under different and known conditions. The essential facts concerning them are that a group of primitive people, as homogeneous as can be expected and well adapted to an environment, was transferred in slavery to different climates and to different social conditions where they interbred with other races, but to some extent remained pure. . . . It is possible with varying degrees of success to compare these people under primitive conditions and under civilized conditions, when comparatively pure and when mixed with other races, when enslaved and when free, when effected by poverty and by favorable economic circumstances, by illiteracy and education, and in rural and urban life.[12]

The American Negro population presents the medical scientist with the opportunity to study disease from numerous different perspectives, Lewis claims, implying that medical researchers do not normally have the opportunity to study disease under such a variety of angles. The American Negro, it would appear, brings the medical researcher close to the ideal setting of the laboratory where, in principle, any particular circumstance or condition can be (re-)produced.

In this respect, then, Lewis's insistence on the suitability of the American Negro as an anthropathological object resonated with the claim made at the beginning of the twentieth century by the African American social theorist W.E.B. DuBois that the United States constitutes an extraordinary "anthropological laboratory," its "Negro" population an ongoing "experiment."[13] DuBois, whom Lewis cites, represents a way of thinking about race, the American Negro, and disease that persisted beyond Lewis and his followers and remains a challenge to any anthropathological project as defined by Lewis.

DuBois's *The Health and Physique of the Negro American,* a little-known but exemplary work, begins with a corrective to the contemporary perception of the "Negro American." "The first and usual assumption concerning this race," says DuBois, "is that it represents a pure 'Negro' type." However, he continues:

The Negro-American [type] represents a very wide and thorough blending of nearly all African people from north to south; and more than that, it is to a far larger extent than many realize, a blending of European and

African blood. . . . In America we have, on account of the wide-spread mixture of races of all kinds, one of the most interesting anthropological laboratories conceivable. This is true also so far as the mingling of the two most diverse races, the black and the white, is concerned as well as in other cases. . . . We have had going on beneath our very eyes an experiment in race-blending such as the world has nowhere seen . . . and we have today living representatives of almost every possible degree of admixture of Teutonic and Negro blood.[14]

As visual proof, DuBois enclosed plates of forty-eight prominent "Negro American" types, detailing their various degrees of admixture. He concluded, based on a series of forty thousand classifications he personally carried out, that one-third of the "Negro American" population was racially mixed.[15]

The overall research program proposed by DuBois in *The Health and Physique of the Negro American* broke new ground. The book is a patchwork of elements taken from physical anthropology, racial histories, migratory histories, miscegenation theories, and vital statistics.[16] Why did DuBois, whose declared intention it was to discuss the health of the Negro American, draw upon such a wide range of nonmedical sources? First, he wished to present Negro Americans, on the one hand, as biologically and culturally distinct from their ancestors and contemporaries in Africa, and, on the other, as constituting a population characterized by its extreme biological, cultural, and socioeconomic heterogeneity. According to DuBois, only a study taking into account these two heretofore unacknowledged facts about Negro Americans could adequately address the issues of health and disease in that population. Second, he aimed to debunk racial formalism, which around the turn of the century was the determining discourse on health and the Negro American. Racial characteristics, in his view, were not fixed entities, the expression of vital essences, or natural laws, as racial formalism would have it, but variables determined by an ever changing environment, by which he meant everything from diet and living conditions to overall cultural and social relations. Third, he aimed to show that no unequivocal causal relationship between race and fitness could be established. Most phenomena identified as "racial" or "pathological," he claimed, are due to social relations within a given social formation: "The Negro death rate and sickness are largely matters of conditions and not due to racial traits and tendencies. [What we have] is not racial disease but social disease."[17]

That DuBois saw anthropology as a liberatory alternative to racial formalism may at a first glance seem curious, given mainstream anthropology's obsession with comparative racial anatomy, biology, and physiology and its centrality to racial formalism. However, DuBois was not a mainstream anthropologist; he actively participated in the formation of a new movement within the discipline, namely culturalism.[18] As we have seen above, this new anthropology challenged the view that races were discrete and constant biological entities, as well as any "racial theory of culture."[19]

The works by Lewis and DuBois represent two views of what the application of anthropology to biology and medicine—and vice versa—may reveal about the American Negro. One instance in which researchers applied anthropathological strategies—as defined by Lewis—was in the search for an explanation of the differential distribution of sickle cell anemia among Africans and American Negroes. My assessment of this anthropathological project is informed by DuBois's insight that race and disease are effects of social relations. More specifically, I will explore how in the 1940s and early 1950s sickle cell anemia became the occasion for the birth of an anthropathology of the "American Negro," and how this enterprise led to the solidification of the notion that the latter constitutes a distinct racial type.[20] I will document a series of instances in which medics[21] relying on information from the anthropological literature used sickle cell anemia to establish the notion of the hybrid and, consequently (in their view), inherently diseased nature of the American Negro. I will also show how sickling researchers with anthropological aspirations gave new prominence to hybridization, which at that point in time had lost its relevance for understanding social relations and human attributes (at least for researchers in the emerging fields of molecular biology and population genetics). In their work, the American Negro was situated at the center of a complex discursive network in which nineteenth-century and early-twentieth-century views on race-mixing and disease gained new prominence as they were aligned with the new disciplines of clinical genetics and biological anthropology.

* * *

Between 1944 and 1953, a debate over the link between race and a specific disease unfolded in medical journals including the *British Medical Journal*, the *East African Medical Journal*, the *Lancet*, and the *Transactions of the Royal Society of Tropical Medicine and Hygiene*, principally among European colonial medical officers stationed in what was then called East and West Africa. Several American medical scientists eventually joined the debate, whose point of contention was the following: Given the fact that the sickle cell *trait* was more common among Africans living in Africa than among African Americans, how could one explain the fact that sickle cell *anemia* seemed to occur almost exclusively among African Americans? The question was all the more puzzling because in 1949 the physicians James V. Neel and E. A. Beet established the genetic distinction between the sickle cell trait and sickle cell anemia: a person who inherits a single gene for a particular genetic variant like the sickling hemoglobin gene (a heterozygous individual) is carrier (in this instance, of the sickle cell trait), whereas a person who inherits two copies of that same gene (a homozygous individual) may contract the condition, here, sickle cell anemia.[22]

Notwithstanding the genetic relation between the trait and the anemia, many colonial physicians and American medical scientists working on sickle cell anemia took the uneven distribution of sickling among "the two major divisions of the black race" to indicate the extent to which diaspora Africans had become a biogenetically distinct population.[23] They considered the biogenetic distinction of African Americans to be the result of hybridization (by which they meant race-mixing), and because this distinction manifested itself in part in the form of a disease (sickle cell anemia), they did not hesitate to propose a link between hybridization and biological and genetic degeneracy. The hybrid American Negro suffering from sickle cell anemia was living proof, they claimed, of the dysgenic effects of race-mixing.

Beginning in the 1920s, physicians in the United States carried out numerous surveys in order to map the geographical and racial distribution of sickling. The surveys revealed that sickling occurred mainly in the South and exclusively among African Americans.[24] (The disease was not found in whites in whom admixture with Negro blood could be ruled out). By the 1940s, however, many physicians had become interested in investigating the global extent of this presumably "black-related" disease. Was it restricted to the United States or could it be found in African populations throughout the Americas as well as in Africa?[25] In their pursuit of an answer to this question, they drew upon existing ethnological knowledge of African peoples and, in doing so, reinforced the fusion of medicine and ethnology[26] which had long been in the making and which would lead to the formation of the discipline known today as medical anthropology.

By 1944, it became clear according to one investigator that "although the American negro population was originally derived from West Africa[,] very few cases of sickle-cell anaemia [had] been reported from these colonies and no account of the incidence of the sickle-cell trait in west African natives [could] be found in the literature."[27] In an attempt to clarify the picture of sickling in Africa, colonial medics made a deliberate effort to examine the blood of native Africans for sickle cell trait and sickle cell anemia. Surveys carried out between 1944 and 1949 reported figures for sickle cell trait between 12 and 27 percent, with some studies suggesting rates of almost 50 percent in certain tribes.[28] These rates for sickle cell trait in Africa were up to three times as high as those for the United States. However, the surveys failed to identify any cases of sickle cell anemia in Africa. The cases that were eventually reported were hardly comparable in numbers to those in the United States; and more important, according to the colonial medics, they involved people who were not (Bantu) Africans: an Arab, an East Indian, and a few whites.[29]

All but a few colonial physicians ascribed the failure to find sickle cell anemia in Africa to insufficient clinical knowledge of the disease and inadequate observation techniques. H. C. Trowell, a physician and lecturer at the Uganda Medical School in Kampala, summarized this view:

There are probably few diseases which are more common in East African Natives, and yet less frequently diagnosed, than sickle cell anemia. . . . The literature does not apparently contain any definite account of sickle cell anemia in a Bantu African. . . . The slow recognition of this anemia in Africa is almost entirely due to the fact that the clinical picture is not clearly visualised, and that it is extremely easy to confuse the disease with malaria.[30]

In contrast, Alan B. Raper, a senior pathologist, and Hermann H. Lehmann, a biochemist, who were colleagues of Trowell's at the

Medical Laboratory in Kampala, Uganda, considered the apparent absence of sickle cell anemia in Africa to be a matter of fact. Acknowledging the high rates for sickle cell trait among Africans, they concluded that "all the reliable evidence suggests that the sickling aberration [sickle cell trait] is much less to be regarded as a cause of morbidity amongst Africans than amongst negroes in the U.S.A."[31] The question was, however, why the "sickling aberration" should cause less morbidity among Africans than among American Negroes. In 1950, Raper posed this question in a paper entitled "Sickle Cell Disease in Africa and America—A Comparison." He wrote that "in many African publications there is to be found the germ of a conviction that the severe forms of sickle-cell disease, and particularly the specific anaemia, are relatively much less common [in Africa] than in the United States." This is so, he continued, "in spite of the much greater incidence of the condition [the trait] in Africa. [And it] is perhaps not wholly due to the greater opportunities for the study of coloured patients in America." He charged that if the anemia was indeed less common in Africa than in the United States," [this] may provide a fresh starting-point for attempts to explain why this hereditary anomaly, so often symptom-less, may at times assume severer forms."[32]

The work that Raper was to carry out on the differential distribution of sickle cell anemia on the African and American continents can be properly understood only in the context of the controversy which up until and throughout the 1940s surrounded the precise relation between sickle cell trait and sickle cell anemia, and the status of the sickle cell trait: Was the sickle cell trait within the realm of the normal, or did it constitute a pathology?

*　*　*

Following James B. Herrick's seminal report on sickling in 1910, a debate erupted over how to understand the fact that sickle-shaped red blood cells, which were usually found in the blood of individuals who had anemia, could also occur in seemingly healthy individuals with no history or symptoms of anemia.[33] Were the sickle-shaped blood cells, involved in the two types of cases (anemia vs. trait), to be looked upon as identical or distinct entities, clinicians inquired; and if they were indeed identical, what was responsible for the varying clinical expressions? Was the presence of sickle-shaped cells in the blood of a healthy individual necessarily a sign of immanent (latent) anemia?[34]

In 1924, V. P. Sydenstricker, a clinician from the Medical College of Georgia, described sickling as a disease recognizable in two phases, which he termed "active" and "latent," depending on the condition of the blood and the severity of the symptoms.[35] The terms "active" and "latent" are commonly used to describe stages of infectious diseases like syphilis. For Sydenstricker and those who used his terminology, the mere presence of sickle-shaped cells in the blood of an individual was a sign that the disease process had entered its initial phase. Hence, even people with sickled blood cells presenting no symptoms of anemia were seen as ill, as it was understood that the disease was already surreptitiously playing its tricks in the cells.

In 1926, the Detroit clinicians Cooley and Lee questioned Sydenstricker's model, contending that "the presence of sickle cells in the blood does not, in itself, imply any essential anemia, active or latent . . . [because] most of the subjects having them are as normal in all other ways as the rest of the coloured population."[36] They proposed that the term "sickle cell anemia" be reserved for "patients with definite hemolytic anemia" and suggested that the term "sicklemia" be used to describe "the condition without symptoms." In their eyes, sickle cell anemia and sicklemia were two separate entities. Having sickle-shaped cells in the blood—sicklemia—should be considered within the realm of the normal for individuals belonging to the "coloured" population. For Cooley and Lee, sicklemia was a marker of the normal "Negro" body, that is, a racial marker, but not a marker of pathology, as it was for Sydenstricker.

In the 1930s, Graham and McCarty, physicians from Alabama, introduced into the discussion concepts from constitutional medicine[37] and eugenics: "Our own impression has been that the sickler who presents even mild anemia is a subnormal individual and even though he may not be regarded as an active case of sickle cell anemia, he is still ill equipped to withstand the vicissitudes of life."[38] The introduction of notions such as the "subnormal individual" marked an important moment in the debate. What had begun as an attempt to come to terms with the appearance of sickle-shaped cells in the blood of healthy as well as anemic individuals became a matter of assessing their constitutional adequacy or inadequacy.

The constitutional approach reached its zenith in the work of

Julius Bauer, a Vienna-born physician and applied constitutional pathologist who eventually became professor of clinical medicine at the College of Medical Evangelists in Los Angeles. In an article on sickling published in 1943, Bauer, with his colleague L. J. Fisher, outlined the situation of "a person burdened with the constitutional sickle cell trait":

Having the sickle cell trait, whether or not resulting in sickle cell disease with or without anemia, he may become the victim of his constitutional biologic inferiority and succumb under circumstances which are innocuous to average normal people. . . . Persons with the sickle cell trait may also have other constitutional abnormalities. In other words, they may be representatives of a "status degenerativus." Such a constitutional state has to be considered as a biological liability, lowering the resistance and adaptive power.[39]

Bauer and Fisher, as well as Graham and McCarty, were persuaded that sickle-shaped cells in the blood of an individual were a sign of constitutional degeneracy.[40] In their view, there was no room for difference within the realm of the healthy, not even at the level of the cell. Rather, they argued, the overall health of the body could be deduced from the state of individual cells, different or abnormal cells being an indication of the abnormality or subnormality of the body as a whole. As they considered the appearance of sickled cells to be determined primarily by "deeply rooted racial characteristics,"[41] they transformed sickling from a mere *marker* of race to a *symptom* of race — more specifically, racial inferiority. Although they succeeded in pathologizing race, they failed to explain why the presence of sickle-shaped cells in the blood leads to sickle cell anemia only in some cases, and what the mechanism responsible for this development might be.

One would expect the work of these early sickling researchers to have lost currency after the genetic distinction between sickle cell trait and sickle cell anemia had been worked out in 1949. Neel's accomplishment should have changed the language in which sickling was being discussed, making the terminology of Bauer, Fisher, Graham, McCarty, and others, as well as the "old" racialist anthropology and eugenics, irrelevant or outdated. In the context of the new genetics, in the manner of Neel and Linus Pauling, one would have expected such terms as race, the Negro (understood as a representative of a racial type), colored people, the subnormal individual, and status degenerativus to have become meaningless and to have been replaced by notions from molecular biology.[42] Indeed, the historian Daniel J. Kevles argues that already in the 1930s and 1940s a "reform eugenics" had emerged which "for the most part was free of its predecessors' patent social prejudice," and he sees the human genetics of the 1950s as purged from racism, classism, and extremism.[43] (In fact, in 1950 physical anthropologists, biologists, and human geneticists said in a UNESCO report — that the concept of "race" had no validity.)[44]

However, historians Garland E. Allen, Nancy L. Stepan, Diane B. Paul, and others have emphasized the resilience of the core beliefs of racialist anthropology and eugenics within human genetic discourses.[45] Paul explicitly cites Neel himself, among others, to show that few human geneticists in the 1950s recoiled from the eugenic enterprise. "What we are really discussing here is a new eugenics, where I define eugenics simply as a collection of policies designed to improve the genetic well-being of our species," Paul quotes Neel as saying.[46] In the 1950s, according to Paul, eugenics and human genetics constituted a continuum rather than two distinct fields. Paul's analysis supports my claim that, in the literature on sickling from the 1950s, eugenics and genetics did not exclude one another, but rather often co-existed or even fused so as to produce a new and powerful racialist anthropology that was informed — and authorized — by the language of molecular biology (especially the discourse on blood group genes).[47]

Although Neel's genetic explanation clarified the way sickling was inherited, it hardly stabilized the boundaries between the normal and the pathological with regard to the sickle cell trait. The debate that followed the findings of the different incidences of sickle cell anemia in the United States and Africa suggested that the issue was not to be solved at the level of genetics. As we have seen, Cooley and Lee, writing in the 1920s, had considered the trait to be within the realm of the normal as far as "coloured people" were concerned. Researchers writing after the publication of the comparative studies of sickling in the United States and Africa came to the conclusion that the trait was indeed a normal phenomenon among Negroes.

The problem remained, however, of how to explain why the "harmless" trait was commonly accompanied by anemia in the

United States but not in Africa. In their search for a solution, researchers focused on the notion that an external agent, perhaps an "infectious agent," was responsible for bringing about the pathological state—using the term "infection" in a very broad sense to designate not only bacterial events, but also social circumstances.

*   *   *

In 1950, A. B. Raper undertook a major review of the African and American literature on sickling, hoping to throw light upon the differences between Africans and African Americans with regard to sickle cell anemia. He began with an acknowledgment that the categories of African and American Negroes reflected not only an ethnological difference but also a biogenetic one. In his preliminary observation concerning the problem of sickling, Raper wrote:

It may be concluded with certainty that the incidence of the sickling trait in Africans is nearly three times that in American negroes. This is a striking difference, and it seems a reasonable inference that the separation of the black race into two groups, African and American, has introduced genetic differences between the two that are of some moment from the point of view of sickle-cell disease.[48]

Raper had his own theory about how this genetic differentiation might have occurred:

In seeking an explanation for the different incidence of the trait in the two major divisions of the black race, we must assume that the forebears of each group were indistinguishable in this particular respect two or three centuries ago, and that it is the less stable community, the American, that has suffered the change. The lower incidence [of the trait] in the New World may have resulted from intermarriage with non-negroes, or, if we allow that fatal complications are for some reason commoner in America, it may be due to a higher mortality amongst sickling families there.[49]

Having ruled out a higher sickling mortality among American families, he continued: "It is therefore suggested as a possibility that some factor imported by marriage with white persons, is especially liable to bring out the haemolytic aspect of the disease, while the anomaly remains a harmless one in the communities in which it originated."[50]

For Raper, the phenomenon of intermarriage was central in accounting for the different incidences of sickling in the Old and New World. The question is, however, how the term "intermarriage" should be read. Raper's explanation may be rationalized in terms of contemporary genetics and biological anthropology as follows: the absence or reduced severity of the anemia in Africans may be the result of a complex of modifier genes in Africa which mollified the diathesis of sickle cell anemia in these less admixed populations. Among African Americans, in contrast, admixture may have disrupted such complexes, making the admixed population more susceptible to the deleterious effects of the sickling gene. From this point of view, intermarriage is synonymous with gene flow and genetic drift.

However tempting it may be to interpret Raper's conclusion in the light of contemporary human genetics, this approach ignores an important dimension of his work. Raper was aware of Neel's genetic distinction between the trait and the anemia but found it to be inconclusive: "Much remains to be done in the way of careful study of the genetics of this interesting and—to the negro—important disease."[51] Raper discussed "genetic differences," but he also used the terms "race" and "intermarriage," and in doing so he situated himself at the intersection of modern genetics and the new physical anthropology on the one hand, and eugenic genetics and racialist anthropology on the other. His concern was not gene flow, but rather the relation between a social practice (intermarriage), its biogenetic consequences (hybridity), and disease.[52]

The fusion of the new technical language of genetics with that of ethnology reinforced the same assumptions that undergirded the otherwise discredited discourse of eugenics.[53] In an attempt to designate African Americans (or more specifically, the hybridized offspring of their intermarriage with whites) as the source of sickle cell anemia, Raper turned his attention to a 1944 study by T. H. McGavack and W. M. German on the Black Caribs of Honduras. These two sickling researchers introduced their project as an attempt to problematize sickling's proclaimed status as a "hereditary racial trait" specific to the Negro population in general:

The presence of sickle cell anemia in people not of the negro race has shown the necessity for careful evaluation of the statement that the disease arises from a hereditary racial trait; and through 30-odd years, the records of one hospital in which Caribs are not infrequently patients fail to disclose a single case of identified sickle cell anemia.[54]

In order to resolve the racial question in sickling, German and McGavack undertook an ethnological investigation of the phenomenon. The case of the Black Caribs, they claimed, was key to determining whether it was justifiable to continue to see sickling as a "hereditary racial trait" specific to the Negro: "The black Carib is a negro of relatively pure strain; sickling has not been studied in the tropics, nor indeed in negroes outside the United States."[55] The ethnological significance of the Black Caribs, according to German and McGavack, was precisely their (relatively) immaculate Africanness, the fact that admixture had had very little opportunity to compromise their "racial essence." The researchers' language is unintentionally revealing:

Carib Indians at the San Juan village, 5 miles from the Tela Railroad Hospital at Tela, Honduras, were subjects of the present investigation. We were fortunate in receiving our introduction to them through one of their number who has attempted some detailed study of their origin. He recognizes 2 varieties of Caribs, the red and the black, and is sustained in this viewpoint by most authorities on the subject. . . . Very little ethnologic consideration seems to have been accorded them. . . . It seems to be fairly well agreed, however, that the progenitors of these peoples came across the Atlantic from Africa, . . . apparently long before Columbus. . . . [Douglas] Taylor describes the intermixture of the black Carib sailor and the Indian woman of the shore he invaded with the resultant development of the type to which the term red Carib has been given. T. Kennedy [a nineteenth-century ethnologist] emphasizes the purity of the black Carib who apparently continued to hold himself apart from any peoples with whom he came in contact. It is upon the blood of the black Carib that the present studies were made. Some knowledge of his customs and moral standards only serves to emphasize the manner in which he has kept himself apart from all other people with whom he has come in contact. The purity of his African ancestry is well demonstrated in the accompanying photograph which is an "at random" picture. His features are characteristically negroid and without resemblance to other Indian tribes of North or South America. There is a heavy head of kinky, wooly, jet black hair. The skin varies in color from chocolate brown to black, more commonly the latter. The forehead is wide; the eyes are keen with muddy yellowish (fatty) deposits in the sclerae; only occasionally are the cheek bones prominent; the nose is thick and flattened; the mouth is large, the lips thick, and the teeth well set and well preserved. Prognathism [protrusive jaw] is not uncommon. Indeed, his resemblance to the African prototype is much more striking than that of his North American brother.[56]

According to McGavack and German, the Black Caribs' resemblance to the African prototype marked them as essentially different from other American Negroes. Displaced to the New World, the Black Caribs, unlike other African Americans, "seem to have preserved wholly their integrity as a colored race."[57] As not "a single case of identified sickle cell anaemia" had been found among the "pure-blooded" Black Caribs, McGavack and German believed that racial admixture rather than displacement (the New World environment) or racial type (being Negro in and of itself) was responsible for the high rates of sickling among their (hybrid) "North American brethren."[58] For McGavack and German, the Black Caribs provided an irresistible opportunity to turn sickle cell anemia into an issue of comparative medical ethnology—what Lewis would call anthropathology.[59]

Drawing on German and McGavack's ethnological observations, Raper suggested that the fact that sickle cell anemia was much more common in the United States than in Africa was indicative of the "less stable" nature of the American community in which the disease appeared. He used "less stable" as an ethno-genetic term referring to relatively higher rates of incorporation of "foreign" genes into a population that in the process was losing its "ethno-racial" discreteness. "The appearance of sickle-cell anaemia," he concluded, "depends not only on the extent to which the trait is present in a community, but also on the extent to which admixture with other genetic strains has occurred."[60] For Raper, then, the absence of sickle cell anemia among the "relatively pure" Black Caribs was evidence enough that admixture between white and black peoples—"a factor imported by marriage with white people"—produced sickle cell anemia from sickle cell trait. Racial admixture and its effects were, in his view, what afflicted African Americans, causing their ills.

By linking disease to "racio-genetic" flux, Raper destabilized the boundaries between medicine and ethnology, making it legitimate to use ethnological knowledge to complicate or resolve quandaries in disease observations. His suggestion that the differentiation between sickle cell trait and sickle cell anemia should be made in the light of a factor such as intermarriage—and not in terms of clinical differences—effectively shifted the focus of the debate from the clinic and its practices to ethnology and its theories about difference. Within this ethnologization of medicine, the high incidence of sickle cell anemia among African Americans came to be seen as evidence of the pathological effects of "racial transgression."

This is not to say that Raper ignored genetics, but rather to point out that the genetics on which he relied was intrinsically linked to ethnological discourse on race. The genetics of the 1950s had not fully extricated itself from the old racialist anthropology when accounting for differences between or within populations. Indeed, many new geneticists sought to do no more than replace the old tools (craniometrics, anthropometrics, etc.) with newer ones (gene frequencies, blood groups, etc.) to reach the same end: a racialist differentiation of people. The new genetics was supposed to have silenced the anthropological discourse on race; instead, the two approaches came to exist simultaneously and interdependently so as to create a gray zone in which researchers on sickling could (and would) easily move from one to the other. Neel's commentary on Raper is a case in point:

> Raper has recently reviewed the literature on sickle cell disease in Africa, and expressed the opinion that the observed paucity of cases of the disease is a real phenomenon and not due to a failure in diagnosis. He advances the hypothesis "that the appearance of sickle-cell anaemia depends, not only on the extent to which the trait is present in a community, but also on the extent to which admixture with other genetic strains has occurred." Paraphrased in the light of current thought on the genetics of sickle cell disease, this would amount to postulating that the genetic balance of the native African is such that the effect of homozygosity for the sickle cell gene is relatively mild; the disturbance of this balance in the United States by intermarriage with Caucasians and American Indians has resulted in an accentuation of these effects. This is a very interesting hypothesis, which certainly must be further explored in the future. However, it does not appear to the present author that the evidence for the failure of sickle cell disease to appear among native Africans is as yet as strong as it needs to be. . . . If sickle cell disease is in Africa the same disease that it is in this country, then some very thorny problems in gene dynamics are raised.[61]

Contrary to what we might have expected, Neel finds Raper's ideas worthy of further exploration, and this in spite of the fact that he considers the evidence presented by Raper to be "inconclusive."[62] Raper's theory about a genetic imbalance in a [human] population brought about by admixture with other genetic strains would, according to Neel, raise "some very thorny problems in gene dynamics." Raper's theory is not compatible with the modern genetic view regarding populations and, by extension, races, because Raper is still operating with the notion of races as discrete entities (each race having its own set of distinctive genetic and other features), whereas modern genetics is concerned with populations that are understood to be groups of interbreeding species sharing the same gene pool. From the point of view of modern genetics, the idea that the human population is constituted of distinct races has no pertinence; racial incompatibility therefore is not a possibility.

Neel was willing to await further evidence from Raper rather than immediately dismissing his theory because, like many other geneticists, Neel still conceptualized certain differences between human groups as racial. Thus far, the racial differentiation of people had been done with reference to external markers; modern (human) genetics, specifically anthropological genetics, however, had given itself the task of providing the hidden markers of race, thus updating and rehabilitating a concept that it could have made obsolete.[63]

*   *   *

Around the same time that Raper was seeking to establish a biogenetic difference between indigenous Africans and diaspora Africans with reference to the differential distribution of sickle cell anemia among the two populations and the varying degrees to which they had been subject to hybridization, physicians in the United States were busy gathering evidence of presumed internal biogenetic differences among American Negroes, also using sickling as a point of reference.

In 1948, P. K. Switzer and H. H. Fouche, two South Carolina physicians, reported that the incidence of sickle cell trait was significantly higher among Negroes of the Charleston area than it was among Negroes in the northeastern United States, which they referred to as "North America."[64] This finding of a geographical difference in the incidence of sickling among African Americans led Switzer and Fouche to speculate on possible ethnological differences within the American Negro population. Echoing Raper, they concluded that "the Negroes in this area ["South America"] represent[ed] a purer strain than those in other regions" "although [they were] descended from natives of West Africa and the Congo, like their counterpart."[65]

In 1950, John D. Hodges, a Philadelphia physician, made his bid in the contest to explain variations in the rates of sickle cell trait and sickle cell anemia among African Americans as a reflection of degrees of racial purity. In the recently founded journal *Blood* he published a study entitled "The Effect of Racial Mixtures upon Erythrocytic Sickling."[66] The task Hodges set out to accomplish was "to clarify the effect of Negro-white-American Indian inter-breeding upon the transmission of this disease [sickling]."[67]

For Hodges, the clarification of the effects on American Negroes of white-Indian admixture involved reconstructing their ancestries. In his view, the African ancestors of current American Negroes constituted without doubt an ethnically heterogeneous group of people and, possibly, a racially mixed one. When Hodges was doing his research, the geographic and ethnic origin of American Negroes had already been established. However, an ethnological classification of the latter was being complicated, he suggested, not only by recent admixture of white and Indian blood, but also by whatever racial admixture might have taken place in the remote past before they were brought to America as slaves.

Hodges begins his study by dating the slave trade to 1619; by indicating that the slave trade was an ongoing practice for more than two hundred years, he wanted to suggest that the ethnic and racial composition of the American Negro population was continuously being modified by the influx of "new blood." Hence, one could not conceive of the American Negro population as stable or homogeneous over time, even leaving aside white-Indian admixture. Hodges then quoted the celebrated African American social theorist E. F. Frazier to insist that "the majority of these peoples were brought from Guinea, Calabar (Niger Delta region), Angola (lower Congo), Gambia, the Congo and a few from Madagascar. [And] most authorities agree that the slave traders sailed, in the majority of instances, from West African ports."[68]

The point of Hodges's preface on the slave trade with its references to the specific locations in Africa from which Africans were captured and brought as slaves to the New World was to argue that the traffic in slaves served to produce in the New World an ethnological reality similar to that known from those African locations. The search for the exact ethnic and racial composition of the American Negro was, for Hodges, a problem of clarifying the ethnic and racial composition of Africa with its many tribes and ethnic and racial groups.

An important influence on Hodges was the clinical pathologist Lemuel W. Diggs and his associates, C. Ahmann and J. Bibb, from the Pathological Institute in Memphis, Tennessee. In a study designed to establish the incidence of sickle cell trait among Negroes and whites in Gainesville, Florida, and Memphis, Diggs turned his attention to "the effect of the mixture of white and negro blood on the incidence of the sickle cell trait . . . by noting the frequency of occurrence of the trait in light and very light negroes as contrasted with dark and black types."[69] Having divided African Americans into these four categories of "racial purity," Diggs, Ahmann, and Bibb showed that sickling occurred more frequently in "light Negroes" than in "dark" or "pure negroid" types. Out of 206 "lightly pigmented negroes," for example, 27 individuals had sickle cell trait, for an incidence of 13.1 percent. In contrast of 701 "deeply pigmented negroes," 51 had sickling, for an incidence of 7.1 percent. "The finding of an apparently significantly higher incidence in negroes with mixed blood than in pure negroid types," the researchers said, "suggests avenues for further investigation," all the more so because "there will come from the interbreeding of the races an increasing number of cases with the sickle cell trait in those apparently white."[70]

The work of Diggs, Ahmann, and Bibb is instructive because they are the first to destabilize the association of sickling with blackness (that is, dark pigmentation) by linking sickling to the "lightly pigmented negroes" and, by extension, to the practice of interbreeding, the mixing of black and white blood, or hybridity. What is at stake in the work of Diggs and his colleagues is the very notion of blackness. Some blacks are more black than others, they claim, and the high rates of sickling among "light negroes" point to the meaningfulness of insisting on this chromatic distinction. The various skin colors the researchers list as indices for degrees of black racial purity were well-established categories when they were writing, owing to the mid-nineteenth-century Southern American racial discourse on blood and purity.[71] By establishing a link between sickling and light pigmentation, the researchers afforded further legitimacy to the categories of light-skinned and dark-skinned Negroes (read admixed and pure Negroes) and the category of the hybrid. The juxtaposition of the diseased light-skinned Negro (the hybrid) and the healthy dark-skinned Negro provided the ultimate proof of the pertinence of the chromatic categories, and, by extension, of the realness and relevance of the notion of the hybrid. Light skin (admixture/hybridity) implies illness, and dark skin (racial purity) means health. Who can argue against a differentiation presented in the irrefutable terms of bodily well-being and dis-ease?

Another influence on Hodges was the British colonial physician and anthropologist C. G. Seligman, who drew an ethnological map of Africa that diagrammed a distribution of African peoples in accordance with the amount of "Hamitic" blood they possessed. (In the nineteenth century, ancient Egyptians, Berbers, and certain peoples of northeastern Africa were referred to as Hamites because they were the descendants of Ham, the son of Noah, according to Genesis.) Hodges discusses Seligman's map at some length:

In the map is shown the distribution of the various groups of peoples in Africa. The "true Negro" was the most accessible to the West African ports and probably made up the majority of those deported to the United States. Seligman describes their physical characteristics: black skin, woolly hair, average stature 68 inches, moderate dolichocephaly [longheadedness], flat broad nose, lips thick and often everted, and frequently a considerable degree of prognathism. [The map] also illustrates the general observation that the African peoples in the regions adjoining the area of the "true Negro" tend to have some admixture of white or Caucasian blood and the amount progressively increases as one travels farther to the north, east or south. It is probable that some people from these adjoining areas were taken as slaves. Some of these persons are tall with noses of medium height, some are short with brown to black hair, brown skin and prominent buttocks.[72]

If Seligman appreciated the fact that some admixture of white or Caucasian blood had occurred in some of the African peoples living in the areas surrounding that of the "true Negro," Hodges was specifically concerned with "the purity or degree of racial admixtures of Negroes and . . . the incidence of sickling in relation to racial admixture."[73] This particular physical-anthropological concern took him well beyond traditional clinical medicine. The study of African racial history was, in his view, as essential as clinical research for an understanding of sickling in the United States.

Hodges used two criteria: "physical characteristics" and "gene-

alogical history" to construct a classification of individuals indexing the amount of admixture present. These criteria were similar
to those proposed by the anthropologist Melville Herskovits, who
in his study of 1,551 African Americans showed a close correlation
between genealogy and physical appearance, using detailed racial
histories and anthropometric measurements. The proportion of
"pure Negroes" in the United States, according to Herskovits, was
22 percent of the overall Negro population.

Embracing Herskovits's strategy, Hodges represented his sample
Negro population as a group of individuals with varying amounts
of white and/or Indian admixture, measured in fractions of eighths.
He thus claimed to demonstrate that:

When the persons are classified as to degrees of Negro from "pure" to
one-eighth, there is a significant variation apparent in the positive group.
*The per cent incidence of persons with sickling is lower in the "pure" Negro and
seven-eighths Negro fractions but higher in the six-eighths and five-eighths fractions.* . . . [Summarizing] the results show that the incidence of sickling
increases with the dilution of the "pure" Negro by small amounts of white
and American Indian blood. . . . [However], the increased incidence is
limited to those mixtures which contain approximately six-eighths or five-
eighths Negro. There is no evidence of an increasing incidence with further dilution by white or Indian blood.[74] (Emphasis added)

Here Hodges presents the dilution of the "pure" Negro's blood
by white and Indian blood as responsible for an increased incidence of sickling. Not surprisingly, he finds the most striking increase in the sickling incidence in people who are five-eighths to
six-eighths "Negro," that is, in the most radically "admixed" (or
"mixed-up") individuals: "It is interesting to note that the study
included fourteen instances of sickle cell anemia and that eight of
these were classified as six-eighths Negro. Not one of the persons
with sickle cell anemia was less than five-eighths Negro."[75] This
confirms his thesis that the "purer" the individual (seven-eighths
to entirely "Negro" or white), the less likely he or she is to be afflicted by genetic abnormalities, and vice versa. In establishing a
correlation between various degrees of admixture with white and
Indian blood and sickling, Hodges's conclusion is nothing short of
a mathematical transformation of Diggs's thesis, which suggested
a link between light pigmentation and sickling. Hodges's work,
based on the law of ancestral heredity, reads like a chapter from

Francis Galton's *Inquiries into Human Faculty* (1883), in which he coined the term *eugenics*.

Soon after Hodges, working within the framework of the old physical anthropology, succeeded in establishing a link between racial admixture and sickle cell anemia, Richard Ashman, a physiologist at The Charity Hospital of Louisiana, drew upon contemporary genetics to complicate and solidify this very association. His work makes obvious the persistence of racialist anthropological and eugenic thinking within the new biological anthropology and human genetics of the 1950s. In an article published in 1952 in the *American Journal of Physical Anthropology*, Ashman states: "From the standpoints both of anthropology and of population genetics . . . sickle cell anemia present[s] interesting and baffling problems." These "interesting and baffling" problems are not of a clinical nature, according to Ashman, as "it appears from clinical studies that the differentiation of trait and disease is not difficult, providing other causes of anemia are ruled out"; rather, they are genetic. Although "from the standpoint of genetic analysis, the mode of inheritance proposed by Neel appears to be satisfactory so far as the situation in America is concerned," according to Ashman, "the problem is to understand how such a deleterious gene could become established in a population."[76]

Ashman then scrutinizes Neel's account of the mechanisms that may be responsible for the establishment of the sickling gene in certain populations (the selective advantage of the heterozygote, a high mutation rate, and genetic drift). Having dismissed Neel's proposals, he states: "It should . . . be clear that, unless one of the proposed mechanisms of establishment of the gene can be demonstrated, a *direct* attack on the problem through the application of the methods of genetic analysis alone cannot afford an answer."[77] More specifically, Ashman proposes "that the disease originated as a by-product of racial mixture."[78] The notion of a disease produced by racial mixture, which was central to eugenics, a discourse on heredity usually associated with the 1920s and 1930s, is somewhat surprising within the genetic discourse of the 1950s, the so-called modern synthesis.[79]

Ashman cites the human biologist J. B. S. Haldane and the serologist A. S. Wiener to supply evidence of the deleterious consequences of racial mixture. Haldane and Wiener had proposed "that erythroblastosis fetalis [hemolytic disease of the newborn] is a consequence of the mixture of Rh positive and Rh negative populations."[80] According to Ashman's reading of Haldane and Wiener, the Rh negative and Rh positive blood groups define distinct populations with specific genetic characteristics that are at odds when these populations are crossed. Because Ashman posits populations as equivalent to races or species he can present rhesus incompatibility as evidence that race-mixing might be dangerous, too.

When Ashman elaborated on his thesis concerning "by-product[s] of racial mixture," he did so with reference to the biologist M. Gordon and the geneticist C. C. Little, who had suggested "the relevance of hybrid studies to human racial mixture in the United States."[81] In order to set up a framework for his project, Ashman turned to the science of animal genetics, where "there are numerous instances of genetic disturbances resulting from the crossing of races or species." Gordon studied a fish, *Platypoecilus maculatus*, that has a sex-linked gene, Sd, which causes spotting at the base of the dorsal fin. If a fish carrying the gene is crossed with another fish, *Xiphophorus helleri*, the hybrids which inherit the gene Sd may have a larger number of pigment cells than the *Platypoecilus maculatus* parent, Ashman observed. "This [is] attributed to melanophore [pigment] stimulating genes in X. helleri." If this hybrid is then backcrossed to another *X. helleri*, some heterozygotic offspring develop tumors in the fin region. "It is evident that gene Sd may be practically lethal in the genotype of another species."[82] Ashman's aim was not to make a statement about these two species of fish, but rather to suggest that the "genetic disturbances" that occur in them when they are crossed might be indicative of similar disturbances in human "hybrids." When he turned his attention to the possible relation between human sickling and hybridity, he used a method of genetic reasoning modeled on animal genetics.

A majority race, which we shall here suppose to embrace nearly all mankind, including the majority racial element in the Negro, has genotype $S_1S_1T_1T_1$. The minority race, supposedly an early population of a part of Africa, had the genotype $S_2S_2T_2T_2$. The genic incompatibility is between S_2 and T_1 and not between S_1 and T_2. We shall suppose that the sickle cell disease appears in individuals having the genotype $S_2S_2T_1T_1$, where the incompatibility should reach a maximum. The trait, therefore, appears in individuals of the genotypes $S_2S_2T_1T_2$, $S_1S_2T_1T_2$, and $S_1S_2T_1T_1$. At the beginning of race mixture, the F1 generation would have the genotype, $S_1S_2T_1T_2$. All would reveal the trait. The F_2 generation would contain the following genotype segregants: $S_1S_1T_1T_1$, 2 $S_1S_1T_1T_2$, $S_1S_1T_2T_2$, 2 $S_1S_2T_1T_1$ (trait), 4 $S_1S_2T_1T_2$ (trait), 2 $S_1S_2T_2T_2$, $S_2S_2T_1T_1$ (disease), 2 $S_2S_2T_1T_2$ (trait), $S_2S_2T_2T_2$. It is at once apparent that when the various trait genotypes are crossed, the observed disease: trait: normal ratio of approximately 1:2:1 will usually not be obtained. There will be a deficiency of the genotype for the disease, $S_2S_2T_1T_1$. However, in the American Negro, trait frequency is only 9%. Therefore, the frequency of the gene S_2 is low, perhaps 0.05. If we adhere to the hypothesis, T_2 will likewise be infrequent, but may considerably exceed S_2 because of past selection against $S_2S_2T_1T_1$ individuals. This would have resulted in a lowering of S_2 frequency and an elevation of T_2. The consequence is that a considerable majority of trait individuals will have the genotype $S_1S_2T_1T_1$, the other trait genotypes being relatively uncommon. Therefore, most trait × trait matings will be between the common trait genotype, and the expected 1:2:1 ratio between disease: trait: normal will occur in the offspring. Mated with normals, the common trait will give the expected 1:1 ratio. Since $S_2S_2T_2T_2$ normals would be extremely rare, normal parents will very rarely produce trait children.[83]

The genetic calculus that Ashman presents appears to concern the modification of genes. A closer look reveals that his argument seems to be based on the presupposition that the notion of races is relevant to genetics because races, like species, constitute distinct genetic types. The notions of "majority" and "minority races" play a prominent role in Ashman's text. Ashman begins by questioning the genetic universality of the majority race (that is, the notion central to modern genetics of a single gene pool shared by all humankind) when he states that the latter is supposed "to embrace *nearly* all mankind." He then goes on to claim that the Negro shares *certain* genetic elements with the majority race, the implied message being that he or she possesses distinct minority genetic elements as well; and that these minority elements constitute the genetic line of demarcation between the Negro and the majority race. The implication of Ashman's notion of "the *genic* incompatibility of S_2 and T_1," then, is that the majority and the minority *races* must be incompatible (because S_2 and T_1 represent "racial elements"). In other words, while appearing to be talking simply about genes, Ashman is making statements about races and race-mixing.

This point is made even clearer in his conclusion:

The theory assumes that in man certain populations had taken a first step in the development of *reproductive isolation* which is responsible for *species formation.* There is no need to go into the manifold implications of the theory in relation to an understanding of the origin of many clinical disorders. If further analysis, observation, or experimentation substantiates the interpretation, it may help in the analysis of the origin of many populations.[84] (Emphasis added)

Here, then, is the fulcrum of Ashman's project: Certain blood dyscrasias (abnormalities of the blood) *are* an effect of racial mixtures. But even more than that, blood dyscrasias (or at least sickling) are useful indicators of the racial origin of certain populations and may be helpful in documenting human "speciation" as a fact, and an ongoing process. Not only is Ashman's thesis at odds with Darwinism—which sees populations as *interbreeding* species—it is incompatible with the population genetics of the 1950s and harks back to the eugenics of the 1920s and 1930s.

Ashman's analysis is valuable precisely because it is characteristic of the 1950s sickling research in supporting racialist and eugenic arguments which by then should have been deemed outdated. While previous researchers, from Diggs, through McGavack and German, and Hodges to Raper, had already drawn a link between racial admixture and sickling, their discussions were, in fact, quickly losing currency from the point of view of the new human genetics (population genetics in particular) that was rapidly forming in the 1950s and constituted the medico-scientific cutting edge. Ashman's "accomplishment" was to rearticulate these old analyses in a language echoing that of the new genetics, thus lending validity to a whole medical discourse on the deleterious effects of interbreeding. Ashman did not present any new evidence but simply recycled existing information within a new interpretive scheme whose principles owed as much to eugenics as to genetics.

Chapter 3
Medical Problems with Ethnological Solutions

The Colonial Construction of Sickling in Africa

According to Michel Foucault, "one of the great innovations in the techniques of power in the eighteenth century was the emergence of 'population' as an economic and political problem." As Foucault saw it, "governments perceived that they were not dealing simply with subjects, or even with a 'people,' but with a 'population,' with its specific phenomena and its peculiar variables: birth and death rates, life expectancy, fertility, state of health, frequency of illnesses, patterns of diet and habitation."[1] More specifically, in Foucault's analysis, modern power, organized around the concept of "population," was (and is) based on "the analytics of sexuality"—that is, on "the management of life" (or sex) through the meticulous regulation and incessant intervention at the level of individual bodies as well as entire social bodies. The analytics of sexuality, Foucault claims, replaced a pre-modern form of power which, resting on the notion of the "people," privileged "the symbolics of blood." Where "sex," in the modern discourse of "populations," is an *object* of analysis and a *target* of intervention, "blood," in the pre-modern discourse of "peoples," was a *symbol* of power, he explains, "a reality with a symbolic function."[2]

Recent events in Europe and Africa and the renaissance of "nationalist," "ethnic," and "tribalist" movements around the world seem to suggest that the pre-modern discourse on peoples defined and differentiated in terms of "blood" has reemerged (if it ever ceased). Although it has not replaced the modern discourse on populations and sexuality, it seems to be interfering with it. What is at the roots of the conflicts in Rwanda, Burundi, and the former Yugoslavia, for instance, if not the fact that the discourse defining these societies as "societ[ies] of blood . . . where power [speaks] through blood" has regained (or never lost) currency.[3] This state of affairs substantiates Foucault's general view that discourses sometimes overlap, interact, and resonate with one another. As to the "symbolics of blood," Foucault explicitly claims that, beginning around 1850, it was commonly called upon to "lend its entire historical weight toward revitalizing the type of political power that was exercised through the devices of sexuality." Most important in this context, he emphasizes the role played by the discourse on blood in the formation of racism "in its modern, 'biologizing,' statist form."

> A whole politics of settlement (*peuplement*), family, marriage, education, social hierarchization, and property, accompanied by a long series of permanent interventions at the level of the body, conduct, health, and everyday life received their color and their justification from the mythical concern with protecting the purity of blood and ensuring the triumph of the race.[4]

An analysis of the pervasive medico-anthropological enterprise of cataloguing the body of the Other and mapping the social structure of Elsewhere seems to substantiate Foucault's point that the discourses of blood and sex have often been—and sometimes still are—coextensive, not least when racialist arguments are being made. Thus, a closer look at what happened in the 1940s and 1950s after colonial medics, anthropologists, and other "blood workers" began turning their attention to sickling within Africa proper, shows that blood was used as a means of depicting groups of Africans as knowable, calculable, and manageable "populations." This proved particularly effective precisely because for these researchers, and their subjects, blood was not only an object of analysis and a target of intervention, but also a reality with a symbolic function.

The reports produced by the sickling researchers whose work will be examined here reveal the extent to which biomedicine, in the context of Africa and Africans, was permeated by other systems of knowledge. Colonial medicine, it would seem, situated Africa and the African body at the intersection of serology, genetics, pathology, and ethnology. Eventually, the normalization of this ethnologizing biogenetic rendering of colonial Africa became a very useful tool in the arsenal already available to colonial administrators in search of "efficient" ways of governing Africans. More specifically, the colonial administration welcomed sickling research because it produced findings that could be used to redefine existing internal divisions of African societies in biogenetic (that is, absolute) terms. Thus, sickling research not only tested and contested existing "tribal" histories and delineations, it became central to the colonial administrative enterprise of rewriting "Native" histories and redrawing social boundaries, an enterprise whose ultimate purpose was to transform the African populace into (more easily) manageable "populations." But as colonial medics began to redraw the lines of demarcation between African collectivities in terms of sickling rates, the term "tribe" was transformed from a social category based primarily on linguistic, cultural, and archaeological criteria to a biogenetic category.[5] Consequently, tribes came to be seen as "naturally" occurring entities within a biogeneticized African social order. Ultimately, then, sickling research in colonial Africa rendered possible the rethinking, in biogenetic terms, of older regimes of truth regarding not only tribal identities, migrations, and histories, but also the origin of the East African Negro, the Asian and European presence in Africa, and the African presence in Asia and southern Europe.

Ironically, the biogenetic discourse on sickling and the ethnology of Africa intersected again and again (and continues to intersect) Galtonian eugenic genetics. Thus, rather than representing a break with the late-nineteenth-century colonial medical discourse on Africa, which privileged such notions as race, purity, stock, and tribe, it resonated (and, in some instances, continues to resonate) with it. This resonance in turn makes the biogenetic discourse on sickling in Africa paradigmatic of the broader colonial (and postcolonial) medical discourse on Africa and Africans. A growing number of scholars are looking at how African colonial medicine constructed difference, in particular "tribal" identities.[6] A case in point is work by the historian Megan Vaughan whose excellent study on colonial power (biomedicine) and African illnesses points out that "biomedical discourse in Africa operated through the specification of the features of groups, rather than the minutiae specification of the features of individuals."[7] (Vaughan uses the term "groups" to refer to what colonial medics called "native races" or "tribes.") Of equal importance here, Vaughan notes, beginning in the late nineteenth century, the colonial medical view of African societies was explicitly eugenic, concerned with "racial purity" and "cross-breeding," and this continued to be so, she claims, well into the twentieth century.[8] More recently, R. Packard and P. Epstein have critically examined contemporary AIDS research in Africa, showing that the "tribalist," eugenic discourse on the African body, disease, and sexuality formulated during colonial times continues to inform biomedical discourses on AIDS and the African populace.[9]

In this chapter I first examine the findings of four sickling researchers working in Africa during the 1940s and 1950s: H. C. Trowell, E. A. Beet, H. Lehmann, and A. B. Raper. I have selected these medics because they are emblematic of the most striking characteristic of colonial medical discourse at this point in time, namely, its tendency to formulate biogenetic issues as ethnological problems and vice versa. I will show how these researchers, in mapping the differential distribution of sickling along "tribal" lines, not only naturalized "tribes" but also ethnologized disease. In the process of carrying out surveys of sickling in Africa, these colonial medical officers displaced sickling from the clinic to the field, so that the phenomenon, which had been seen primarily as a clinical concern to be addressed in terms of treatment, cure, and prevention, came to be viewed mainly as an ethnological tool helpful in answering heretofore open questions about the migration history, racial "purity," and the origin of various "tribes."

I then discuss the work on sickling carried out by Lehmann and various colleagues in India and other parts of the world during the 1950s and 1960s, documenting how sickling became central to the explicitly and exclusively ethnological enterprise of establishing a "racial" link between Africa and India, a project which ultimately would entail the rewriting of the ancestral history of the East African as well as of the relationship between the latter and the "true Negro" of the West African forest region.

*   *   *

In the mid-1920s, Thomas B. Cooley and Pearl Lee, two American pediatricians from Detroit who were well known for their work on sickle cell anemia (see Chapter 1), proposed a project for medical practitioners in Africa: "Might not men working in Africa, where the negro strains are still well separated, perhaps find a tribe in which sicklemia is the rule?"[10] Much can be gleaned from this question, which is emblematic of its time in many interesting ways.

First, the inquiry is informed by the discourse of "racial" distinctiveness and purity which dominated medico-anthropological thinking in the late nineteenth and early twentieth centuries. Second, it echoes the idea, predominant in ethnological circles as well as in the popular imagination at the turn of the century and beyond, that Africa constituted a kind of primordial reality;[11] that is, in this context, a place where, as opposed to the Americas (the New World), at least some native races, or "negro strains," had remained uncontaminated by admixture. An important implication of this conceptualization of Africa as an instance of the past (characterized by racial "purity") in the present (where miscegenation reigns) is that the African body was deemed likely to hold the key to the true racial and biological nature of its derivative, the Negro body (that is, the diasporic African body). Sickling among American Negroes could not be fully understood, it was implied, until an account of sickling among Africans had been made. According to the same discourse that articulated "Africa" as a kind of museum of natural history where one could go to seek out past realities, including "non-evolved" human forms and social formations that had long been extinct elsewhere, American societies constituted anthropological laboratories (in the manner articulated by W.E.B. DuBois as mentioned in Chapter 2) where human forms and social formations underwent constant metamorphoses and where, consequently, the truth of the origins was irretrievably lost.[12]

Third, the question resonates with the colonial administrative discourse on the African social which, early in the twentieth century, in conjunction with ethnology, systematically elaborated and promoted the category of the tribe as a means of governing—or rendering governable—the African people. For Cooley and Lee, writing in the 1920s, "tribe" was a transparent term that one could use without qualification when referring to the individual units making up African societies. Historians and anthropologists have pointed out, however, that the tribe, far from being the original (precolonial) African social form, was an effect of colonialism, more specifically of indirect rule, a form of British colonial administration in equatorial Africa at the beginning of the twentieth century.[13] As the historian John Iliffe aptly puts it: "The British wrongly believed that Tanganyikans [and other Africans] belonged to tribes; Tanganyikans created tribes to function within the colonial framework."[14]

Last, Cooley and Lee's question is instructive because of the linkage it establishes between tribes and blood. In the 1920s, when sickling researchers spoke of sicklemia, they were referring to the presence of sickle-shaped cells in the blood, that is not necessarily to a medical condition (clinical symptoms) but rather to a particular status of the blood that could be documented through laboratory tests. By suggesting that "men working in Africa" search for "a tribe in which sicklemia is the rule," Cooley and Lee made a case for the use of blood as a valid marker of tribal identity. Thus, they joined ranks with those who would naturalize ethnological entities (such as "tribes") by defining them in biological terms. More specifically, they followed the lead of the serologists of their day who used blood types to divide populations into "racial" groups.[15] Sicklemia, in the view of Cooley and Lee, was yet another particular type of blood that could be used to establish racial distinctions between people. Their statement exemplifies the extent to which medicine and ethnology were intertwined, epistemologically and sociopolitically, during the first two decades of this century.

In 1926, the date of Cooley and Lee's statement, there was one reported case of sickle cell anemia in Africa which involved an Arab boy from the Sudan.[16] No surveys of sickling in African populations had been carried out, so what allowed them to envision the existence of an entire African tribe in which sicklemia was the rule? Because sickling is found among African Americans and constitutes a racial trait, their reasoning went, and because the African American population originated in Africa, sickling must exist in Africa and among Africans. It is clear, then, that their rendering of sickling as a likely problem for Africa and Africans owed nothing to concrete clinical evidence and everything to ethnological speculation.

The colonial medics who eventually studied sickling in Africa seem to have taken Cooley and Lee's challenge strictly to the letter. They pursued the phenomenon primarily as an ethnological matter, exploring mainly what sickling (blood) could reveal about tribal histories, differences, and identities as well as about the very origin and true bioracial nature of "the African."

*   *   *

In 1945, the *East African Medical Journal* carried an editorial entitled "Sickle Cell Anaemia," introducing a paper of the same title by H. C. Trowell, a physician and lecturer at the Uganda Medical School in Kampala. The significance of Trowell's paper, according to the editorial, was that it was the first to document in a systematic way that "a comparatively new form of chronic haemolytic anaemia"—sickle cell *anemia*—constituted a considerable medical problem in Africa but had "passed unrecognized, because unknown, in many an African hospital and for many a long year."[17] In the article that followed the editorial, Trowell reported finding thirty-five cases of the anemia distributed among seven East African "tribes." Earlier researchers such as R. Winston Evans had documented the existence of sickling among "West African Natives" but did not distinguish between sickling as a clinical phenomenon (sickle cell anemia) and the appearance of sickle-shaped cells in the blood (which does not necessarily produce any clinical symptoms and whose exact status was therefore highly contested).[16] Until Trowell's report, the significance of sickle cell anemia in Africa had been subject to intense debate, many medics leaning toward the belief that the phenomenon did not present a problem there in so far as only a handful of sporadic cases had ever been documented. But now that Trowell had shown that sickling did indeed exist in Africa, the editorial seemed to be saying, the perception that sickling was absent from that continent must be seen as a result of the inadequacy of the diagnostic criteria available to—and the ignorance of—the medical researchers working there. Even after Trowell published his findings some researchers remained skeptical, claiming that in spite of their heightened awareness of sickling and protracted efforts to identify new instances, they had been unable to document more than a few sporadic cases.[19]

The editorial is also, in a general way, emblematic of the colonial medical discourse on sickling in Africa:

[Sickling] was first recognised no more than twenty-five years ago in African negroes in America; but as the X-ray examination of the skulls of Mayan Indians from Mexico, dating back to hundreds of years ago, has shown evidences like those found in the skulls of sickle cell patients today, one may assume that this form of the anaemia has really a history reaching far back into the past. And sickling has been observed recently in Mexicans; the vast majority of the cases reported so far have been found in America, and it is of interest to note that a very similar condition of the blood has been discovered in deer.[20]

Acknowledging the clinical importance of sickle cell anemia in contemporary Africa, the author of the editorial is just as intrigued by the fact that Trowell's findings further refine the disease map of Africa past and present. In general, colonial medical discourse and practice was characterized by emphasis on identification and classification (as opposed to treatment) of diseases and on the usefulness of disease in identifying and classifying people.[21] The editorial, characteristically, moves from the clinical via the ethnological and the historical to the zoological(!). This suggests that the colonial medical discourse on phenomena specific to Elsewhere and Others did not restrict itself to clinical medicine. In other words, colonial medical researchers, in discussing Africa (as opposed to the West), did not extricate the clinical realm from other realms of knowledge, particularly not those of ethnology and ethno-history. As a consequence, their clinical investigations were also always ethnological enterprises.

Trowell, in one of the first epidemiological investigations of sickling to be carried out in Africa, drew a map showing the migratory movements of Africa's populations from south to north into "Arab countries" and from North Africa further north into "southern Europe." This map, he claimed, quite easily explained the occurrence of sickling in places outside of Africa:

Since Bantu slaves were freely taken into Arab countries, the Sudan and also Egypt, and since the sickle cell trait is probably a Mendelian dominant, it follows that some cases of this disease should be found in these countries. Indeed, since African slaves travelled freely to the southern European countries, where they became absorbed into the general population, it is not surprising that six out of the seven cases in Europeans have been in Greeks, Italians and Sicilians.[22]

If Trowell saw the occurrence of sickling in Arab countries and southern Europe as posing few or no problems in that it was a direct result of an easily identifiable ethnohistorical factor, namely the "free travel" of (that is the free trade in) African slaves, he had no such simple answer when it came to the differential distribution of sickling within the African continent.[23] In his view, sickling within Africa represented a higher level of obfuscation. This was so because the notion of "the freely travelling African slave," which obviously translated as "infusion of Negro blood into Caucasian populations" or "miscegenation," and as such explained sickling in the Americas and southern Europe (see Chapter 2), seemed to have no pertinence in the context of Africa and Africans. How could there be miscegenation if there were no distinct races to be mixed? As I have shown in the two previous chapters, the term "Negro," when occurring in an American context, always designates a nonwhite (as opposed to "black") individual. It implies an order of things which is based on the distinction between whites and others. In a context that is perceived to be exclusively "black African" the term thus defined has no relevance. It seems that there can be no African equivalent of the American Negro—the hybrid—but this is not so. The colonial medical researchers who eventually "made sense" of sickling in Africa did so with reference to the so-called Hamitic thesis, according to which physical variations among African peoples reflected true racial differences—more precisely, the extent to which various groups had been infused with the blood of the "pastoral Caucasians" known as the Hamites, that is, with "white" blood. Some Africans were defined as more "white" than others, and the term Negro came to designate the "true Negro," that is, the African free of Hamitic or "white" blood.[24] In such a context, the admixture thesis would once again have currency.

To be sure, Trowell remained uncertain about the adequacy of the term "Negro" for the description of the ethnological realities of Africa: "The term Negro does not correspond closely to any ethnographic unit [in Africa], [even though] it connotes the descendants of the Bantu tribes of West Africa."[25] The problem, as Trowell saw it, was primarily whether or not the anemia existed in Africa, but it was also a matter of visualization, by which he meant the process of establishing a relation between the phenomenon and a particular racial body. While he contended that "the slow recognition of the anaemia in Africa is . . . due to the fact that the clinical picture is not clearly visualised, and that it is ex-

tremely easy to confuse the disease with malaria,"[26] Africa's social
and racial diversity—the myriad of tribes, the complex dynamics
of intertribal and intratribal relationships, the multiple physical
variations—also complicated the picture of sickling in his view. Implicit in his writings, then, is the idea that no clear understanding
of sickling in Africa was possible until an adequate account of the
confusing African social fabric and racial makeup had been made.

*   *   *

After Trowell and others[27] acknowledged that the internal ethnological divisions of Africa would make any attempt at accounting for sickling on that continent quite difficult, E. A. Beet, a
medical officer and specialist in tropical medicine and hygiene
working at the Colonial Medical Service of Northern Rhodesia
(Zambia), placed sickling at the center of a whole new medico-
ethnological semiotics of blood. Beet's work had considerable implications for colonial administrative practice. By mapping the differential distribution of the phenomenon among various African
peoples, Beet's work made possible not only the redrawing of heretofore commonly accepted tribal lines but also the rewriting of
well-established tribal histories, thus rendering "governable" heretofore "wild" and "unruly" populations.[28]
    Although both Trowell and Beet considered the systematic
screening of Africans seeking treatment at colonial hospitals to
be the appropriate way to gauge the extent of sickling in Africa,
Trowell did not situate the practice of screening within a broader
ethno-historical context to the same extent as Beet. Even though
Trowell meticulously noted the tribal affiliation of the patients he
screened, this information remained a mere notation, his main
objective being to show simply that sickling occurred in Africans.
Beet, while similarly screening the blood of people seeking medical treatment at the hospital where he was working, was concerned
with more than merely documenting the presence of sickling in
his African patients. One might say that his work began where
Trowell's left off. Thus, from its inception his study engaged the
predominant ethnological discourse on the physical and social environment that constituted the "natural setting" of his patients,
and he took into consideration the social space in which sickling
existed outside of the hospital (and the individual body), thus link-

ing the phenomenon not only to certain geographical locations but also to certain tribes.[29]

In 1946, Beet published the results of a major survey on sickling from the Balovale district in Northern Rhodesia. Beyond the fact that it further documented the existence of sickle cell anemia in Africa, this report is interesting because it raised many of the questions that defined the debate on sickling in Africa in the 1940s and 1950s and up until today: the origin of the phenomenon, its differential distribution among tribal (and more recently ethnic) groups,[30] its relations to malaria and other kinds of anemia, and its relevance for defining a norm for the African body.

Beet presented his project as "an investigation . . . into the incidence of the sickle cell trait among the local Bantu population," noting that "no work on this subject ha[s] previously been carried out in this District."[31] Characteristically, he began his report by describing the geography of the area:

The Balovale District of Northern Rhodesia is in the Kaonde Lunda Province of that Territory. The Province occupies the north-west corner of Northern Rhodesia, and Balovale is the most westerly of its three Districts. . . . To the north and west of Balovale is Angola, the boundary to the north running parallel to latitude 13° south and that to the west parallel to longitude 22° east; running approximately through the centre of the District from north to south is the Zambesi River. The southern boundary is formed by the rivers Lungwevungu and Kabompo which flow into the Zambesi from the west and east respectively; to the south is the Barotse Province of Northern Rhodesia. The eastern boundary is formed by the Manyinga River which flows into the Kabompo, the latter continuing in a southerly direction and then turning sharply to the west.[32]

He then offered a short characterization of the people who inhabited the district, insisting on their almost complete isolation from Europeans ("civilization"):

The African population of the District is about 60,000 men, women, and children; the European population is very small. . . . Balovale must be one of the most rural areas remaining in east Africa, the people coming into contact with Europeans only through one of the three missions and the Government Boma staff (which consists of two Administrative Officers and one Medical Officer). The nearest point on the line of rail in Northern Rhodesia is at Chingola, 480 miles away from the Boma over very bad roads, and there is only a sporadic lorry service which connects the two; the railway in Angola is much nearer being only 300 miles distant, however, there are no roads going from Balovale into Portuguese Territory. An area such as this presents ideal conditions for the study of any disease, particularly one, like sicklemia, known to be of a familial nature.[33]

From the outset, Beet, the physician, situated his project at the intersection of geography, ethnology, and medicine. A geographically well-defined rural (read "primitive") region, the Balovale District, whose inhabitants had very little contact, if any, with the outside world (were uncontaminated by civilization and miscegenation), would be a site of choice for any classic ethnological investigation. For Beet, this controlled environment with its isolated and therefore authentically indigenous inhabitants was akin to a museum and an ethnomedical laboratory. It "present[ed] ideal conditions for the study of any disease, particularly [those] . . . known to be of a familial nature," as he stated, because it offered the medical researcher the opportunity to observe a given disease process in a significant but finite number of persons who were situated in a social and physical space that could be known in its entirety because of its circumscription; who, because they were Other, could be dealt with through the specification of the features of the group, as Megan Vaughan puts it, rather than through the detailed specification of individual features;[34] and who could be treated as human specimens. As a field laboratory, the Balovale District made possible the visualization of disease in geographical and ethnological (tribal and kinship) as well as in medical terms, an approach Beet deemed crucial for the understanding of a "familial" disease such as sickling.

Examining blood from 815 consecutive in-patients attending the Government Hospital at Balovale, Beet calculated a sickling incidence of 12.9 percent, which "represent[ed] the District as a whole" as cases were drawn from all areas.[35] These figures, he pointed out, compared well with those found elsewhere in Africa.[36] However, Beet continued, only one case of classical sickle cell anemia was seen. As anemia, whatever its cause, is one of the most common afflictions besetting the African body, he explained, "it is hard . . . to assess the amount of any anaemia due to sickle cell disease."[37]

Beet next divided the Balovale District into seven areas, lettered A to G. He claimed that these areas were marked out "on a geographical basis, rather than on a scheme based on tribal distribution, as the population is concentrated along the banks of rivers and streams."[38] In spite of his claim that his map was drawn solely on a geographical basis, Beet had already demonstrated his engagement with ethnology in a previous sentence, where he described the people resident in the areas in question as "being of adjacent chiefs."[39] It is clear that Beet strategically appropriated geography as a metaphor for the social. Ethnology, in particular its concern with tribes, remained, even when he explicitly denied it, the organizing principle of Beet's research. This is what makes his perspective paradigmatic of the colonial medical enterprise.[40]

The fusion of geography, ethnology, and medicine, in addition to producing knowledge that might be helpful in treating or curing disease, generated information about African society, including its "tribes" and the origin of the African. Beet's general account of the distribution of sickling within the Balovale District reads as follows:

Most of the cases came from area A, as this is a heavily populated part of the District (of about 13,000 to 14,000 persons) and the Government Boma of Balovale is situated in the middle of it. By far the greater part of the population resides to the east of the Zambesi River (45,000 out of a total of 60,000) and this accounts for the greater number of patients examined from areas A–E inclusive.[41]

Beet seems to be saying that the distribution of sickling in the Balovale District can be explained by the law of frequency—the more people, the more cases. He notes later in the article, however, that "area F which occupies the west bank of the River throughout its length has a very low incidence, compared to all the others and is obviously in a class by itself."[40] In order to explain the discrepancy between the sickling rates identified for the east and west sides of the river, Beet turned to ethnohistory:

This interesting distribution of the sickle cell trait among the people of the District can be explained by studying tribal history; area F is occupied by the Lovale tribe but to the east of the river are resident the Lunda and other tribes, the Lunda being predominant. In 1890, there was the Lunda-Lovale war and up to this time, and for some time afterwards, there was not much mixing of the two tribes. In 1907, the Government Boma station was opened at Balovale and from that time onwards there was a tendency for the Lovale to move across the river and to mix with the Lunda, either as individuals or as family groups, but no similar migration took place by the Lunda into Lovale territory. All this is confirmed by the distribution of sicklaemia. Originally the sickle cell trait must have arisen, in this District, in the people living to the east of the Zambesi. As time passed the incidence of this condition must have arisen gradually to its present figure; but, owing to the lack of movement from east to west, sicklaemia never became established to any extent in the Lovale tribe, with the result that today two Bantu tribes are living adjacent to each other with a marked difference in their sickling rates. Apart from the Lovale living in Northern Rhodesia there are members of this tribe living across the border in Angola, from this group. It is at once apparent that there cannot have been much mixing of these two sections of the same tribes, in the near past, as there is a considerable difference in their sickling rates (3.5% and 11.4%). It is known that, apart from the Lovale emigration to the east already referred to, the Portuguese Lovale have also been moving into the areas A–E, with the result that now there are considerable numbers of the Lovale living there.[43]

Extricating an ethnostatistical profile of sickling from his examinations of the inhabitants of the Balovale District, Beet rendered the latter as a population consisting of subgroups that were internally differentiated in terms of their respective sickling rates. In other words, using the parameters of the physical and social environment, he made of the Balovalens well-defined units of analysis (populations) and as we shall see (more easily) manageable and manipulable objects of colonial administration (tribes). The remainder of Beet's argument further illustrates this point:

It was decided to use the figures obtained for the distribution of sickle cell trait in the District to determine the composition of the Lovale people who have emigrated into the land adjacent to the east bank of the river; the knowledge thus obtained would be *useful* as it would enable one to get an idea of the amount of alien emigration that has taken place, in recent years, into the east-central portion of the Balovale District. To do this the natives examined from areas E, A, and West B were classified by tribes, it was found that the Lunda and Lovale were the most numerous and so attention was devoted to these two only. Of the 220 Lunda from here 34 were sicklers giving an incidence of 15.5%, of the 120 Lovale 20 were sicklers giving an incidence of 16.7%. The rate for these Lovale is considerably greater than that for their fellows across the river in Northern Rhodesia (3.5%) but is similar to that found among the Portuguese Lovale (11.4%). This shows that the emigration of Portuguese natives into the area concerned has been considerably greater than any movement of the Northern Rhodesia Lovale into the same area. Therefore, it can be concluded that there is now a considerable alien population resident within the boundaries of the Balovale District.[44] (Emphasis added)

Why would it be "useful," as Beet claims, to know "the amount of alien emigration that has taken place, in recent years, into the east-central portion of the Balovale District"? It is important here to problematize the apparently transparent term "useful," situating it within the context of colonial administration. In order to do so, we need to take a closer look at the ethnohistory of the Balovale District and its people relied upon by colonial administrators of the 1940s.

Most ethnohistorical accounts of the Luvale and Lunda peoples in the Upper Zambesi depict them as remarkably similar in material culture, sharing a historical tradition, with enough linguistic similarities to make communication relatively easy and intermarriage common.[45] Despite the many features perceived by ethnologists as linking the two groups, the Zambesi District of the 1940s and 1950s was a place of continuous strife, as witnessed by the numerous states of emergency the authorities declared.[46]

To explain the tension between the groups, ethnohistorians commonly refer to the "tribal" history of the Balovale district. Robert Papstein, a historian who has done extensive work on the Luvale-speaking peoples of the Upper Zambesi, for example, explains that, in 1907, when the Balovale Boma opened, the Luvale and Lunda found themselves under the administration of the Lozi "chief" Lewanika. The latter had struck a deal with the British South Africa Company (BSAC), which had the right to administer all of Bulozi and its dependencies. The BSAC placed Balovale, as it was then called, under the auspicies of Lewanika, who had convinced the BSAC that the Upper Zambesi was part of the Lozi domain. The Luvale and Lunda joined forces to fight Lozi encroachments, presenting their cases to the local authorities. However, at the same time the British, Portuguese, and Belgian colonial governments drew borders between their respective principalities, an agreement that effectively distributed the Luvale and Lunda groups among Northern Rhodesia, Angola, and the Congo Free State.[47]

Although the Luvale and Lunda cooperated in resisting Lozi sovereignty, their relationship continued to be marred by tension, a situation which made it difficult for the colonial administration to govern them effectively. Therefore, in 1923, the District Commissioner Bruce-Miller attempted to end the strife between the two

groups and bring about administrative order by requesting that
the Zambesi River be used as a dividing line between the Luvale
and Lunda. According to Papstein, "the use of the river as a tribal
boundary would have resulted in the bulk of the best arable land
in Chavuma [the area straddling the Zambesi where it flows from
Angola into Northern Rhodesia] falling under Lunda authority
when, by all accounts . . . Chavuma was a predominantly Luvale
area."[48] The Lunda supported this plan, their alliance with the Luvale against the Lozi notwithstanding. But it also meant that the
Luvale residing in the Chavuma, an ethnically heterogeneous area
since the late eighteenth century, had to be relocated. The Luvale
resisted all attempts at relocation, and eventually violence erupted
between the Luvale and Lunda groups, resulting in the abolition
of the policy. Nevertheless, according to Papstein, "the use of the
Zambesi as an administrative border . . . was so compulsively ap-
pealing that virtually all District Commissioners attempted to em-
ploy it. . . . It became an article of faith among subsequent District
Commissioners that the Luvale belonged 'properly' on the Zambesi's west bank and the Lunda on its east bank."[49] Papstein continues: "Commitment to this point of view, reflected in the formu-
lation of subsequent policies, has been the single most important
stimulus to tribal strife between Lunda and Luvale. Every local
political decision was—and still is—evaluated in terms of whether
it would further or diminish each side's claim to the Chavuma, the
area's best agricultural land."[50]

Beet read the results of his research as pointing to the potential of sickling (genetics) to resolve these tribal conflicts, hence his
reference to the usefulness of his findings. He concluded his report by stating that "an investigation of sickle cell disease in an
area may confirm beliefs about recent tribal movements, and thus
assist investigators interested in tribal history."[51] Beet also invited
C. M. N. White, the District Officer of Balovale, to comment on his
findings and conclusions. White, himself a fledgling ethnohisto-
rian of the area, remarked:

[T]he final conclusion—that very few of the Lovale now living east of the
Zambesi came from west of the river, but in actuality came from Angola
for the most part—is the most unexpected result of this study. It had
always been assumed that the Lovale on the east of the river had come
from the west of the Zambesi, and political tension between the Lunda
and Lovale has been frequently centred around this assumption. No de-

tailed investigation of the origin of the Lovale now residing east of the Zambesi has ever been made, however, and in view of Dr. Beet's finding, an investigation of this nature should be undertaken when opportunity offers since definite information upon this point would have *administrative value*.[52] (Emphasis added)

White, who clearly shares Beet's view that sickling research can be used to rewrite the history of peoples (tribes) under colonial administration, is saying here that the relationship between the Lunda and the Luvale is marked by "political tension" caused by, among other things, the "assumption" that the Luvale is an alien population originating in the area west of the Zambesi. However, he continues, the results of Beet's investigation indicate that the Luvale living on the east side of the river do not originate on the west bank but rather in Angola. According to White, then, the implication of Beet's findings is that the "political tension" between the two tribes is based on a false assumption about the origin of the Luvale. In other words, White considers tribal politics in the Balovale District to be based on an incorrect version of the area's tribal history. White welcomes Beet's findings because they provide his administration with an opportunity to correct, on a biomedical basis, the version of history informing the intertribal conflicts of the day, a correction which, it is implied, will definitively settle these conflicts and render governable the unruly Lunda and Luvale: hence the "administrative value" of the findings.

In colonial Africa of the 1940s there was nothing new about using ethnological knowledge to administrative ends.[53] In 1935, for example, G. Gordon Brown, an anthropologist, and A. Bruce Hutt, the District Officer of the Iringa District (Tanganyika Territory), published *Anthropology in Action*, a book that examined, in the authors' words, "to what extent anthropological knowledge can be made applicable to problems surrounding the administration of an African tribe."[54] In his foreword for the book (with which he was involved from its inception), Sir Philip Mitchell, the Chief Secretary of Tanganyika Territory, specifies that it is an account of "practical experiment in co-operation between a District Officer administering his District and an anthropologist."[55] He continues:

You [A. Bruce Hutt] and Brown agreed with me that there would be valuable experience to be gained from a practical attempt to solve the difficulty [of combining taxing administrative duties with academic study] by linking specialist [anthropological] research to the day-to-day business of administration, in a manner which might be compared to the relation between *laboratory worker* and *practising doctor*, and that an attempt of this nature would have to be confined in the first place to a limited field and to proceed experimentally towards the discovery of methods capable of general application.[56] (Emphasis added)

Mitchell then goes on to describe the task awaiting the team of the anthropologist/District Officer:

The task is twofold, and may be summarized in two questions: (1) is the local government based on tribal loyalties and traditional authority, deriving from the past, acceptable in the present, and, as far as can be judged, capable of appropriate development to meet future conditions? and (2) are the people well governed and content?

The first step might be to obtain a general historical account of the tribe, its origins, traditions, and organization, to be followed by a description on the broadest lines of the political, economic, and social conditions in which it finds itself to-day, and the administrative structure, British and native, set over it. A comparison might follow of the old tribal hierarchy with the existing administrative and judicial organs, showing differences and if possible accounting for them.[57]

What makes Mitchell's views relevant in this context is not only his belief that the results of anthropological research can be fruitfully put to administrative use but also his juxtaposition of the anthropologist and the District Officer, on one hand, and the laboratory worker and the practicing doctor on the other. For this alignment of professions reflects how ethnology, colonial administration, and medicine can no longer be extricated from one another; and thus defines the discursive field within which Beet situates his work and from which it derives its significance.

When sickling became implicated in the colonial enterprise of rendering governable the social environment of Africa, tribes began to be addressed in biomedical terms. Sickling research as it unfolded in Beet's work brought together what was known about disease, early African tribal history, ethnology, and linguistics. But the categories of ethnohistory, ethnology, and linguistics that identified past vestiges of tribes and current tribal groups had been complicated by the emergence, in their midst, of the biomedical technologies of blood. To the external criteria of similarity and difference had been added a criterion from the archives of the body—the blood-picture (sickling status) of individual tribesmen. The tribe, in other words, had been naturalized (or racialized).

Beet regarded his medico-statistical findings as being of immediate relevance to the colonial administration of the Lunda and the Luvale, and more precisely, he perceived the truth about these groups' origins and their right to land to be speaking through their blood (as objectified by biomedicine) rather than through their own rendering of the past. Sickling, in his view, was a most reliable means of identifying tribes "when the other stigmata of [their] descent ha[d] disappeared,"[58] that is, of maintaining the notion of "tribal" difference even when no ethnological or political difference could be established.

Beet would ask why very high rates of sickling were identified for some groups of Africans while significantly lower rates were found for others residing between them. Such a question could not be answered, of course, by the naked data produced through the screening of blood in the laboratory. Rather, a concurrent study of the contacts and relationships defining African social space seemed to be called for.[59] For this reason Beet eventually shifted his laboratory from the clinic to the field.[60]

One of the issues confronting colonial medical researchers attempting to make sense of disease in Africa was the fact that a norm for the African body had not been established. One thing seemed obvious to them, however: the standards that applied to the African body were not the same as those defining the European body. Among Africans, for instance, parasitic infestations and anemia appeared to be common, making the "normal" African body a malarial and anemic body. Further complicating the establishment of a bodily norm for the African was the fact that African bodies, in the discourse of colonial medical practitioners, were always categorized in terms of their perceived tribal affiliation. Once the tribe was established as defining African social reality (just as race is today in the United States), the notion of a generally valid norm for the African body became difficult to maintain. If, for example, the members of two or more tribes inhabiting the same geographical area had different sickling rates, how could one uphold the notion of a bodily norm that transcended tribal boundaries? Blood, in general, and the sickle cell trait, in particular, played a crucial role in the making of the "normal" African body.[61]

In 1949, taking advantage of a health survey of Lala school children in the Serenje District of Northern Rhodesia during which all the children were tested for the sickle cell trait, Beet sought to demonstrate "how the trait behave[d] in a pure stock Bantu tribe."[62] The incidence of the condition among this group was 13.6 percent (42 of 308 children possessed the trait). He went on to investigate the families of certain children: "family trees were drawn up and every individual who could be contacted was tested for the trait; this entailed visits to many villages and in a few cases medical officers elsewhere were requested to trace and test certain persons who had moved to their areas."[63] Based on his analysis of four family trees, Beet showed that of the offspring produced by the mating of a sickle-celled subject with a "normal" one about 50 percent would be heterozygous; and that of the offspring produced by the mating of a sickle-celled subject with another sickle-celled subject at least 75 percent would be homozygous. He concluded that sickle cell trait behaves as a Mendelian dominant, and suggested that sickle cell anemia occurs in homozygotes only.

At first glance, Beet's analysis seems to fall squarely within the realm of Mendelian genetics. Insofar as it is about a population and its specific characteristics such as its state of health in general and its sickling rate in particular, it can also be viewed as an example of the analytics of sexuality as posited by Foucault. Indeed, by the time Beet got around to examining them, the Lala schoolchildren had already been visualized as a "population" in that they had been the object of a health survey and their bodily attributes and deficiencies had been inscribed through the quantifying techniques of the survey. Beet continued the project of visualization initiated by the survey by registering the details of the genealogies of a select group of the children (those who were found to possess the sickle-cell trait and whose families "were reasonably accessible").[64] Based on the family trees thus produced, he carried out the analysis of sickling and "mating" which eventually led him to the "discovery" of the genetics of the phenomenon, and for which he was credited, independently of James V. Neel, in 1949.

Although a comparison of Neel and Beet would lead me well beyond the bounds of this immediate project, some revealing differences exist between the discourses they drew upon to arrive at their similar conclusions. Neel's approach was defined by the emerging clinical and population genetics. He proceeded by moving from the clinic into specified "populations" and then immediately returning to the clinic. Sickling, to him, was an object of analysis as well as a target of clinical intervention (diagnosis, counseling, and treatment). A closer look at Beet's study reveals that, unlike Neel, he was not concerned with the clinical implications of his findings. Rather, the centrality afforded to concepts such as purity, stock, and tribes betrays Beet's engagement with Galtonian (eugenic) genetics. More precisely, Beet had not extricated himself from the particular way of seeing that Foucault labeled the symbolics of blood. In Beet's work, the concern with "purity," "stock," and "tribes" remained instrumental in the production of knowledge. As a result, sickling ultimately emerged as less of an individual or collective health issue, and more of a powerful biogenetic tool in the ethnological enterprise of writing identity and difference.

It is important to note here that Beet was working in Africa whose opacity, in the eye of the colonial outsider, never ceased to inspire and then complicate attempts at making sense of its social and political relations. Neel, in contrast, carried out his work in Detroit, among African Americans and Italian Americans who were seen as well-defined populations; he was operating within a social realm that was perceived as posing no problems of categorization to be resolved. In general, Beet's work, like that of most other colonial physicians, was ultimately determined by the broader colonial discourse on African societies according to which the latter was of an essentially "obscure" nature and as such invariably challenged and complicated attempts to shed light on its internal organization. This, in turn, meant that Beet's work, like most colonial medical work, had to be primarily a project of visualization: to make sickling visible, to make it emerge from the obscure (social) environment that was Africa. Through his work on the Balovale District with its limited and isolated population, for instance, Beet visualized sickling, first, by accounting for the phenomenon in ethnological terms (along tribal lines), then by using it to problematize the very ethnological categories (tribal demarcations) underpinning his initial analysis. Thus Beet's work, while making sickling visible, also illuminated some of the principles (migration and tribal expansionism) organizing African societies. This simultaneous investment in medicine and ethnology makes Beet's studies emblematic of the colonial medical enterprise in Africa.

*   *   *

If the practice of formulating ethnological problems as "blood matters" (biogenetic issues) was initiated by colonial medical practitioners like Beet, it became fully realized in the work of the physician and chemical pathologist Hermann Lehmann (in collaboration with a succession of colleagues).[65] From the mid-1940s through the 1960s, Lehmann published reports on an impressive number of investigations, all of which addressed the ethnological significance of sickling, in particular its role in assessing racial origins and admixture at the level of populations. Early in his career, Lehmann had been a staunch defender of the view that sickling was "an essentially Negroid feature."[66] Around 1953, however, due to the accumulation of counterindicative evidence from outside Africa, in particular South India, he came to the conclusion that sickling was not restricted to the Negro race. This did not mean that he stopped viewing sickling as a marker of race; rather, from then on, his work focused on the use of sickling rates as a means of affirming racial kinship between various populations, in particular certain South Indian and East African tribes.

In the late 1940s, Lehmann and A. B. Raper carried out a survey of sickling in Uganda with the intention of mapping the incidence of the sickle cell trait ("sicklaemia") in that protectorate. They published their findings in *Nature* (rather than in a strictly medical journal), thus addressing an audience to whom their observations must be presumed to have been of "academic" (speculative) rather than clinical interest. More specifically, according to the authors, the publication of their findings reflected "a wish to . . . indicate how our results bear on physical anthropology."[67]

Lehmann and Raper presented their project of recording "tribal incidences" of sickling in Uganda as owing everything to the specific ethnological configuration of the protectorate: "Uganda lies at the point of contact of several ethnological groups, in particular the Hamites, Nilotes and Bantu. Thus widely differing tribes could be studied within a comparatively small area."[68] Upon examining nearly 5,000 persons from the Protectorate—"about 1 in 1,000 of the population," Lehmann and Raper divided "their" population into three main language groups ("Hamitic," "Nilotic," and "Bantu"), each consisting of tribal subgroups "in which the incidence of sicklaemia [did] not differ significantly between the various groups composing the sub-group." [69] However, they went on to state, "[b]etween any two sub-groups of a given language-group . . . the differences in incidence [were] statistically significant." [70]

So far, Lehmann and Raper had done little more than present the "tribal incidences" of sickling in Uganda. It soon became clear, however, that they perceived their findings to be relevant to the very specific — and far more ambitious — enterprise of determining the origin and true tribal identity of African peoples. Although Lehmann and Raper did not cite the ethnological work that provided them with the information about Uganda's tribes and their respective distinctive features (language, physical type, customs, social form), they were clearly informed by the late-nineteenth- and early-twentieth-century ethnological and archaeological representation of Africans, crystallized in the discourse of racial history.[71] This discourse defined Africa as a continent without history or civilization and its people as existing "in nature." Although all African societies were primitive from a racial historical point of view, they represented many forms of social organization, with which ethnologists and archaeologists had to come to terms. The solution favored by early racialist historians was to promote the sinister notion of progress as embedded in another teleological concept, that of social evolution. They articulated the theory that cultural evolution in Africa was contingent upon the highly developed "Hamitic" race's passing on its traits (civilization and intellectual advancement) to an inferior race, the (black) Africans, through infusion (of superior blood). It was this "Hamitic" thesis that guided Lehmann and Raper's analysis of their survey of sickling in Uganda.

Lehmann and Raper's discussion of the physical anthropological significance of their study substantiates this point:

Unlike the two previous groups [the Hamitic- and Nilotic-language groups], a wide variation is seen among the Bantu tribes. *The incidence of sicklaemia appears to be inversely proportional to the contact the various tribes have had with their most recent Hamitic invaders.* Thus the trait is least common among the Bairu, who have lived for generations as helots [serfs] to the ruling class of Hamitic conquerors, the Bahima, on the best pastoral land in Uganda. Next come the Banyaruanda, Banyoro and Batoro, whose traditions and customs testify to prolonged contact with the Bahima, and whose aristocracy possesses Hamitic features. The contact of the Baganda, Bakonjo and Barundi with Hamitic peoples in recent times has probably

been less direct and made by way of their neighbours, the Banyoro, Batoro and Banyaruanda.[72] (Emphasis added)

By stating that the incidence of sickling is "inversely proportional" to the contact any given tribe has had with its "Hamitic
conquerors," Lehmann and Raper situated their discussion within
the context of a debate that had long been absorbing archaeologists, biologists, and linguists about the true identity of the Egyptians, the nature of their relation to the Nubian people, and to the
peoples inhabiting sub-Saharan and Southern Africa.[73] Without
going into the details of this debate, we must mention at least one
of its participants, the physician and anthropologist C. G. Seligman, who formulated the "Hamitic thesis."

By the mid-1920s, Seligman had become the principal spokes-
man for the thesis depicting Egypt as a zone of racial mixture. He
had effectively grafted onto Carl Meinhof's classification of the
languages of Africa (with its physico-typological and evolutionist
overtones) A. C. Haddon's racial classification (which attributed
an absolute value to each racial stock), thereby turning Meinhof's
linguistic term "Hamite" into an all-encompassing "racialist" term
describing not only a linguistic characteristic but also a specific
physical type and social form said to be "Caucasoid." Comment-
ing on the term "Bantu" which he considered to be designating
not only linguistic features but also physical ones, he claimed that
it was where Bantu and non-Bantu tribes were next to one another
"that certain physical qualities [were] to such a degree characteristic of each linguistic group that within particular areas a terminology based on language also serves to differentiate physical
groups."[74] One of Seligman's contributions to the racial history of
Africa, then, was the naturalization (or racialization) of the linguistic criteria used by ethnologists in delineating tribes.

In a series of works spanning some thirty years, and culminating
in a now classic publication—*The Races of Africa* (1930), Seligman
outlined a racial theory according to which the majority of Africa's
peoples—with the exception of those of the West African forest
regions, the home of "the true Negro"—are "Hamiticized" to a
greater or lesser extent. His theory would explain, he claimed,
the variation in skin color and cultural and intellectual sophisti-
cation among the peoples living in the Nile valley, revealing why

darker skin and cultural "primitivity" became more prominent as one moved from the northern to the southern part of the valley. This phenomenon, Seligman stated, was no mere happenstance of nature but rather reflected the extent of the contact any given "dark agricultural Negro" population had had with "better armed" and "quicker witted" "pastoral Caucasians," namely, the "Hamites" and their "superior" blood and culture:

> The mechanism of the origin of the Negro-Hamitic peoples will be understood when it is realized that the incoming Hamites were pastoral Caucasians—arriving wave after wave—better armed as well as quicker witted than the dark agricultural Negroes, for it must be remembered that there was no Bronze Age in Africa. . . . Diagrammatically the process may be described as follows. At first the Hamites, or at least their aristocracy, would endeavour to marry hamitic women, but it cannot have been long before a series of peoples combining negro and hamitic blood arose; these, superior to the pure Negro, would be regarded with disdain by the next incoming wave of Hamites and be pushed farther inland to play the part of an incoming aristocracy vis à vis the Negroes on whom they impinged. And this process was repeated with minor modifications over a long period of time, the pastoralists always asserting their superiority over the agriculturalists.[75]

Lehmann and Raper were clearly informed by Seligman's Hamitic thesis when they concluded that the sickling incidence of any given tribe is an indicator of the extent to which that tribe has been infused with "Hamitic" blood, a low sickling incidence indicating substantial admixture of "Hamitic" blood and a high incidence indicating "pure" or "purer" Negro stock. By situating their work within the framework proposed by Seligman, they also implicitly linked high rates of sickling and pure Negro stock to sociocultural primitivity. Ultimately, Lehmann and Raper legitimized the Hamitic thesis by bringing "hard" serological evidence to its support. In the words of their colleague R. Elsdon-Dew, they provided Africanists with an "absolute method" for assessing the degree to which various "Negro" populations had been subject to admixture of "non-Negroid" blood.[76]

Lehmann and Raper did not share in Seligman's attempt at naturalizing language by identifying correspondences between linguistically and physical anthropologically (or serologically) defined groups of Africans. Rather, they used their findings to problematize, if not rectify, delineations of tribes based on linguistic criteria, showing that linguistic similarities often hide physical (or serological) and, therefore, it is implied, "truer" differences:

The incidence of the sickle-cell trait is uniformly low in the pastoral, Hamitic-tongued tribes, with the single exception of the Teso. The latter, however, have not the Caucasian features of Hamite stock; they are a largely agricultural group, settled amid and intermingling with Nilotes and Bantu. *Their possession of the sickle-cell trait in considerable intensity is an additional physical character distinguishing them from the Hamitic group with which they have been classed on a linguistic basis.*[77] (Emphasis added)

Although the Teso constitute a "Hamitic-tongued tribe," Lehmann and Raper say here, their non-Caucasoid features indicate that they are not true Hamites. This suspicion is confirmed by the fact that they are found to possess the sickling trait—a Negroid feature—"in considerable intensity." Lehmann and Raper continue:

The Nilotic tribes, according to the Uganda handbook composed of the Gang, Bari and Madimoru speakers, are remarkably homogeneous with regard to sicklaemia, excepting only the Madi (on the Sudan border). *The Lango, who live between the Acholi and the Teso, appear from our findings to fall uncompromisingly within the Nilotic group. This is of interest because the presence of some Teso words in their language has been used as evidence that they are in reality a branch of the Teso who have adopted an easier Nilotic language.*[78] (Emphasis added)

Having demonstrated how the distribution of the already racialized sickle-cell trait can be used to test and, by extension, confirm or contest "tribal" and "racial" histories constructed according to presumably less definitive linguistic and physical anthropological criteria, Lehmann and Raper suggest that sickling surveys be viewed as a more "refined" and "reliable" ethnological tool. They conclude: "We consider that, so far as Central Africa is concerned, a study of the distribution of sicklaemia could usefully contribute to physical anthropology."[79]

*   *   *

Following his work on the ethnology of sickling in Uganda, Lehmann began an ethnological classification project that eventually took him across four continents (Africa, Asia, Australia, and

Europe). Thus, sickling research became an international enterprise. What unified global and local research on sickling was the organizing principle. In both instances the results were meant to (1) support or refute existing tribal or ethnic delineations based on less absolute linguistic, archaeological, and (oral) historical criteria; and (2) identify the geographical and racial origins of various populations. Lehmann's project might be seen as an attempt at applying the "absolute method" of genetics to validate Seligman's Hamitic thesis worldwide rather than on a strictly African scale.

In 1952, Lehmann published with Marie Cutbush a seminal study on sickling in southern India. Why there? The fact that sickling had been found in one East Indian individual from South Africa (as noted in Chapter 2) could hardly justify such a potentially enormous undertaking. Lehmann and Cutbush rationalized their enterprise as follows: "When the traveller in East and Central Africa inquires from the inhabitants about their distant past, they will often tell him of tall men, fairer than themselves, bearded and with long hair, who came from afar bringing codes of law, handicrafts, and cattle."[80] This kind of narrative was not, according to Lehmann and Cutbush, "pure myth," but had been substantiated by archaeological investigations showing that "the broad-shouldered skeleton of the modern Bantu appears only in Neolithic excavations, whereas the types found in older strata are more slender."[81] The term "slender" here is a clear reference to Seligman's "pastoral Caucasians" and attests to Lehmann and Cutbush's engagement with his Hamitic thesis. "Fortunately for anthropologists," Lehmann and Cutbush continue, "present-day inhabitants of Africa possess distinctive features in their blood—the sickle cell trait, a very high incidence of a particular combination of Rh antigens known as Ro (cDe), and another blood-group antigen provisionally referred to as He."[82] These distinctive features of the blood could prove useful in testing (that is contesting or confirming) the East African tale of "tall," "fairer," and "long haired" invaders: "It seemed possible that an investigation of the blood of certain Southern Indian communities might serve to refute or support the idea of a racial link between Africa and India."[83]

But the South Indian population, like Africa's, challenged classification, for it, too, was divided into a myriad of "ill-defined" collectivities or tribes. In Lehmann and Cutbush's words:

There is no general agreement how the peoples of South India should be classified. They have in the past often been divided into settled communities, or Dravidians, and aborigines, or Pre-Dravidians, but there are objections to this on both linguistic and cultural grounds; nor does the division correspond clearly to anything in the history of these populations. The Pre-Dravidians of the Nilgiri Hills vary from civilized agricultural communities such as the Badagas (who have affiliations with the Canarese) to tribes such as the Irulas, Kurumbas, and Paniyans, who are found living under primitive conditions in the jungle.[84]

In southern India, a variety of communities represent varying levels of "civiliz[ation]" and can not be easily divided into "tribal" categories on linguistic, cultural, or historical grounds. Nevertheless, Lehmann and Cutbush have no difficulty designating "the aboriginal tribes . . . as the group in whom, a search for African blood features appeared most likely to yield positive results."[85] An examination of the blood of the aboriginal Badagas, Todas, and Irulas (with that of the Tamils, Malayalis, Canarese, and Telegus serving as controls) revealed sickling rates of 30 percent, 8.4 percent, and 3.3 percent, respectively, in the first three communities; the last four registered zero. As to the incidence of the Rhesus antigen Ro (cDe), Lehmann and Cutbush calculated a low level similar to that found for Europeans and northern Indians. According to the authors:

These findings lend support to the idea of an Indian migration to Africa in prehistoric times. The reverse possibility—an influx of African blood bringing the sickle-cell trait to the hills of Southern India—should have resulted in a raised incidence of the gene combination Ro (cDe). The fact that the incidence of Ro is high everywhere among the negro races of Africa, whereas the incidence of the sickle-cell trait shows wide variations among them, suggests that Africa received the sickle-cell trait at a period too recent to allow an even distribution over the continent.[86]

The outcome of blood studies from South India seemed to provide the serological evidence needed to validate the tale of "tall," "fairer," and bearded men coming to East Africa from the east (Asia), bringing with them "civilization" in the form of "codes of law, handicrafts, and cattle." And this new "evidence" was not of an inconclusive archaeological nature; rather, it had been found in the blood of the contemporary descendants of those whose migratory lives were presumably summarized by the Hamitic thesis— the prehistoric "Veddids," an aboriginal people of India.

In another version of their article that appeared later in 1952 in the *Transactions of the Royal Society of Tropical Medicine and Hygiene*, Lehmann and Cutbush expanded their discussion. Drawing upon E. von Eickstedt (a German nineteenth-century ethnologist), they divided the Dravidian-speaking people of southern India into three racial groups:

> The North-Indids and Indids, to whom . . . belong the Coorgis, Canarese and the Telegus.
>
> The Melanids, who like the Indids are "Europoids" in physical features, but have a deeply pigmented skin. (The Tamils are included here.)
>
> The Veddids, the oldest inhabitants of India, who to this day belong to the most primitive communities of all mankind.[87]

Of these three races, only the "Veddids" were found "to harbour the sickle-cell trait which suggests a relationship with Africans."[88] This finding resonated with that of the South Asian anthropologist B. S. Guha, from the Indian Museum in Calcutta, who reported in a series of articles that he had found "Negrito Racial Strains" among "the Kadars, Pulayans, and Malsers of the Cochin Hills in Southern India."[89] More specifically, according to Lehmann and Cutbush's survey of the various Indian "communities" (the Paniyans, Irulas, Kurumbas, Badagas, Toda, Canarese, Telegus, Malayalees, and Tamils), sickling rates were very high (31 percent) in the three communities belonging to the "Veddid race," zero among the Melanids (Tamils), and in the single digits among the Indids (Badagas) and North Indids (Todas). They saw this as an indication that sickling, in India, was linked to "primitivity" (as had been the case in Africa) and low social status. The Veddoids, they stated, "live either as food gatherers in the jungle, or, where they have been absorbed into the Indid society, have been given the lowest place in the caste system."[90]

Lehmann and Cutbush also used their findings to establish a relationship between sickling and a particular set of physical features described as "non-Mediterranean," "Veddoid," or similar to those of the "East African Negro": "The Veddoids showed the ridges of the eyebrows, the broad base of the nose, the wide mouth and the weak chin we had seen in the arch type of the forest Negro in East Africa."[91]

Not surprisingly, then, Lehmann and Cutbush ultimately read their findings as linking the blood of South Indians to that of East

Africans, thereby "throw[ing] light on the racial history of India itself":[92]

In Africa such high values [of sickling among the Veddians] are found only in those few Bantu tribes which have no living memory of migration and claim to be autochthonous in the back waters of the migratory stream of East Africa: the Basoga in the swamps of the Upper Nile, the Bagishu at the foot of Mount Elgon and the Babullibulli and Bamwezi in the tropical forests at the foot of the Mountains of the Moon.[93]

An important implication of Lehmann and Cutbush's findings, as they saw it, was that the notion of the sickle-cell trait as an essentially "Negroid" feature could not be maintained:

The trait seems to have entered Africa from the north-east, has been spreading southwards and westwards, and seems still to be in the process of establishing itself. *While measurement of Rho frequency may be used as a "tracer" of African ancestry, the sickle-cell trait cannot be used for that purpose.* Even the assumption that the occasional sickle-cell-trait-carrier found in Italy and Greece must have inherited the gene from an African forebear can no longer be maintained.[94] (Emphasis added)

Lehmann and Cutbush also problematized Raper's idea that Europeans inherited the sickling gene from Africans:

Most Veddians are found today in South India, but pockets have been described in Persia and in the Hadhramaut which brings them to the former land bridge between Asia and Africa in the region of Aden. . . . *Veddian blood may have found its way into the Mediterranean peoples*: Cipriani reported Veddian skull features in the Sardinians of today; small dolichocephalic people were discovered among the remains of predynastic Egypt and the piriform opening of the skulls of the children found in the Grimaldi cave in Monaco has Veddian features.[95] (Emphasis added)

While Lehmann and Cutbush refuted the commonly accepted view of sickling as restricted to the Negro race, they did not question the existence of racial features and continued to see sickling as a marker of racial affinity. Their study had provided evidence in support of the idea that the sickling gene had been imported to Africa from Southern India and had established, in the absolute terms of serology, a link between the "Veddoids" of southern India and East Africans, thereby calling for the rewriting of the racial history of the latter. The East African Negro, as they saw it, did not originate solely in West Africa, as Seligman had believed, but also in Asia, as suggested by the anthropologist L. S. Leakey: "The present East African population is a mixture of the high Ro non-sickling Bushmen type with Veddoids bringing R2 and sicklaemia as their contribution."[96]

After the India study, Lehmann and his various colleagues pursued sickling and blood group frequencies around the world for the sole purpose of testing and, when "sufficient evidence" was produced, rewriting racial histories. As part of this project they eventually examined the racial identity of the Achdam of South Arabia, "a dark-skinned people with Veddoid features"; a group of Australian aborigines "in which a strong Carpentarian ['Veddoid'] component prevail[ed]"; the "not entirely tame" "Negritos" of the Andaman Islands in the Indian Ocean (the Onge) who, based on blood type findings, were linked to the "Oceanic Negro"; and the Sicilians, southern Italians, and Greeks, in whom the sickle cell trait was no longer a valid tracer of African ancestry, since Lehmann's own India research with Cutbush seemed to have shown that the presence of the trait in Mediterranean peoples could be the result of an infusion of "Veddoid" blood.[97]

*   *   *

In this chapter I have sought, through a focus on the published reports of several colonial medics working in Africa during the 1940s and 1950s, to examine the role of sickling (and by extension the broader spectrum of colonial medical and political rationalities) in the colonial construction of African social relations and "the African." Medicine and ethnology became inextricably linked in this endeavor, and although professional anthropologists have been almost absent from my analysis to this point, anthropological terms and approaches are ubiquitous in the reasoning of the "blood workers" whose work I discuss.

When professionally trained physical anthropologists finally became involved in sickling research, in the mid-1950s, they added little that was new to the discussion. Like the colonial medics who preceded them, they were interested in sickling mainly as a research tool helpful in "refining" specific anthropological knowledge about given tribes. In 1951, the anthropologist A. C. A. Wright, who was then the honorary editor of *The Uganda Jour-*

nal, commented on the work of Lehmann and Raper. He began quite modestly by introducing to those outside the profession the ethnological significance of certain advancements in medical science: "Those unconnected with the medical profession . . . [should know] that recent research has developed methods for detecting in human blood a wide range of factors which . . . are a promising addition to the data which the ethnographer may use in attempting to classify communities."[98] These methodological inventions are valuable, Wright is saying, because

> hitherto students of ethnology and local history have had to depend for indications of tribal movement and cultural contact (prior to the arrival of written contemporary records) upon such misty mediums of interpretation as oral tribal tradition, and upon observed similarities or differences in language, social structure and cultural artifacts. Now it seems that within the reach of comparatively simple field research there are available two independent methods [sickling and blood group referencing] for testing communal affinities.[99]

Wright believed that ethnologists needed not only to appropriate these two methods but also to improve on them, as they moved their research to a second level:

> In order to save time they [Lehmann and Raper] did . . . tend to use artificial aggregations of population, such as hospital patients, station labour gangs and prison inmates, for the taking of samples. The next stage, now that tribal percentages in sickle-cell trait have been shown to differ significantly, is to carry the range of blood comparison down to the point where the component communities of each tribe are the subjects of study rather than the tribe itself. It may thus be possible to resolve a number of apparent inconsistencies in the records obtained to date, and to go much further towards checking oral tradition as to movement and miscegenation. It is obviously desirable that such a study should be carried out as soon as possible, before the effects of economic migration blur the whole picture and before the old men, who still retain oral traditions of the clan genealogies and of the movements and relationships of the pre-European era, disappear.[100]

The project Wright outlines here—the use of serology for "checking oral tradition as to movement and miscegenation"—was already under way in the work of the colonial medics he cited. Nevertheless, it was taken up by a number of physical anthropologists, including Ronald Singer of South Africa. In 1953, in a seminal review of the literature on sickling, Singer proclaimed that "the anthropologist's main interest in the blood of the African Negro groups lies in its genetical and ethnological significance as borne out by the sickle cell trait."[101]

Not all anthropologists, however, followed the path of Wright and Singer, and by the mid-1950s, there were two predominant anthropological discourses on sickling. One presented the phenomenon as shedding light on migration and miscegenation issues; the other articulated sickling as an instance of natural selection in humans.[102] This bifurcation of the anthropological discourse on sickling did not disrupt what had clearly become the tenacious metanarrative of sickling as a means of cataloguing and regulating African social relations (tribes) and assessing in (absolute) serological terms the origin and racial composition of modern Africans.

The natural selection approach owed as much to colonial medicine as did the migration-miscegenation discourse. A. C. Allison, in 1954, first put forth the notion that sickling might be an instance of natural selection in humans.[103] Traveling throughout the British colonies, he had long been involved in the colonial medical project of drawing blood and establishing racial and tribal affinities. Privy to the malaria association's findings over the years, he eventually marshaled the available evidence to advance the hypothesis that carriers of the sickle-cell trait were immune to malaria.[104] Sickling, according to his hypothesis, was the only example of human adaptation to the environment.

Contrary to what one might have expected, Allison did not see the malaria thesis as incompatible with the existing ethnologizing discourse on sickling. After all, not only was he familiar with the ethno-anthropological practice of using sickling to determine origins, movements, and degrees of miscegenation; he actively participated in the discourse that defined it. Indeed, as he organized his target population along tribal lines he observed what others already knew, namely that "great differences in the incidence of the sickle-cell trait among different tribes are apparent."[105] For Allison, the malaria thesis was an attempt to account for what the ethno-anthropological discourse on sickling left unexplained: "The anthropological interpretation of sickle-cell trait distribution in terms of ancestral origins does not attempt to explain why the sickle-cell gene should remain so common over such a wide area in spite of the constant elimination of genes in persons dying of sickle-cell anaemia."[106]

Allison demonstrated the seeming continued validity of the anthropological discourse on sickling in specific cases such as that of the Hamitic-speaking Teso:

Lehmann and Raper's generalization that the Hamitic tribes have the lowest incidence of sickle cells is true, but these people are as a rule pastoral nomads living in [a] country relatively free of malaria. On the other hand, the Teso are a Hamitic-speaking tribe living in an area where malaria is prevalent, and their incidence of sickling is comparatively high; but this particular tribe might possibly have a considerable admixture of blood from nearby Nilotic peoples with a high incidence of the trait.[107]

Allison concluded by stating:

Lehmann and Raper's view that the incidence of the trait in the Bantu tribes is inversely proportional to the degree of Hamitic admixture is not supported by my own observations. It seems that the effect of environment, in particular malarial severity, is more important than the effect of racial admixture upon the frequency of the sickle-cell gene in East Africa."[108]

Although Allison identified shortcomings where he found them, he never discredited outright the anthropological notion of racial admixture, and hence, the Hamitic thesis.

After Allison had successfully used sickling to render visible that which human biologists had made endless claims about (well before any instances had been documented)—that our bodies, far from having finalized the transition from nature to culture (or to paraphrase Claude Lévi-Strauss, far from having commanded Nature to go no further in the presence of Culture), the biological anthropologist Frank B. Livingstone used sickling to find a rather different connection between human culture—as opposed to environmental determinism—and disease. In 1958 Livingstone argued that culture was the principal mediating factor between the environment and the human body and that sickling was an effect of this cultural mediation. Marshaling data from West Africa, he showed that "the cline in the frequency of the sickle cell trait coincides with [the] spread of yam cultivation."[109] He argued that a particular agricultural practice—slash-and-burn—was responsible for opening up the dense forest and thereby exposing a largely agricultural population to malaria-carrying parasites:

> The agricultural revolution has always been considered an important event in man's cultural evolution, but it also seems to have been an important event in man's biological evolution.
>
> . . . Two results of the agricultural revolution seem to account for this change in the role of disease in human evolution: (1) the great changes in the environment, and (2) the huge increase in the human population. Both of these seem to be involved in the development of holoendemic malaria. . . . First . . . [i]t is . . . possible that the parasitization of man by *P. falciparum* is due to man's blundering on the scene and causing the extinction of the original host. Second, concomitant with the huge increase in human population, this population became more sedentary and man also became the most widespread large animal. Thus, he became the most available blood meal for mosquitoes and the most available host for parasites. This change resulted in the adaptation of several species of the Anopheline mosquito to human habitations and the adaptation of many parasites to man as their host. Under these conditions, holoendemic malaria and probably many other diseases developed and became important factors determining human evolution. . . . *The sickle cell gene thus seems to be an evolutionary response to this changed disease environment. Hence, this gene is the first known genetic response to a very important event in man's evolution when disease became a major factor determining the direction of that evolution.*[110] (Emphasis added)

In the authoritative history of sickling, Livingstone's thesis has become the textbook account. It is usually implied that the sickling field came into its own only when the sickle-cell gene was identified as "an evolutionary response" to a "changed disease environment," and that a sense of closure was achieved thereafter. This became clear to me several years ago when a physician-biochemist friend of mine told me that, as far as he was concerned, the last word on sickling had been spoken, and that the only thing left to do was to fix the cell problem.

Is sickling today a purely mechanical matter to be resolved at the level of the cell? Probably not. In 1989, long after the last colonial medics exited the field, and well after modern biochemistry and molecular genetics arrived with their assurances that they were uncontaminated by politics, Livingstone, in what amounted to a review of the contemporary literature on sickling, begins his discussion as follows:

There has always been the implicit belief that sickle cell anemia is a disease that occurs only in Blacks. This is undoubtedly due to a large extent to the fact that it was first discovered in a Black American and that the overwhelming number of cases in the United States occur in Blacks. When cases are found in whites, they are assumed to be due to racial admixture; and since these cases occur primarily in Mediterranean populations this seems plausible.[111]

Livingstone starts with a disclaimer, which seems to indicate that he is intent on getting beyond the notion that sickling is a racial disease. The fact that this notion must be addressed at all points to the continued effectiveness — or power — of the anthropological discourse of racial disease. As Livingstone continues his assessment of the literature, it becomes clear that, in the context of sickling, the anthropological register has lost none of its force:

The distributions of the B^s gene in Africa and of the three major haplotypes in Africa reflect to a remarkable extent the major diffusions of Arabic influence into Africa. In Senegal most of the contact was with Morocco and Algeria, while in Nigeria Arabic influence and even Arabic tribes came from the Sudan to Bornu, and in East and Central Africa it came from along the East African coast. The populations with low B^s frequencies are those with the least Arab contact or influence. The situation in India looks different in that many of the most primitive tribal peoples have the highest B^s frequencies. However, these populations have the most severe malaria, and Muslim populations are found throughout the areas of India where the B^s gene is found. If the Arab expansion has carried the B^s gene throughout these areas, then this diffusion has occurred in the last approximately 1,300 years, or about 50–60 generations. This is faster than anyone has imagined or estimated, but it does seem possible given the very high fitness of the heterozygote and the great amount of gene flow that has occurred among these populations.[112]

As tempting as it might be, to insist on the similarities between Livingstone's "gene flow" and Lehmann and Raper's Hamitic admixture thesis would inevitably obscure more than it would reveal. The conditions of possibility of the two discourses lie in different epistemological arrangements, even if the discursive fields they define seem similar. Nevertheless, their affinity attests to the continued pertinence of the symbolics of blood in the practice of classifying and managing people.

The final point I wish to make is that when it comes to the Elsewhere which is Africa and the Other who is the African, there is (still) no discourse that does *not* at some point intersect with those of anthropology and ethnology. The discourses of biochemistry and molecular genetics are no exceptions. By way of a conclusion I offer the following programmatic statement by A. D. Adekile, a Nigerian medical researcher, writing in 1992: "The molecular biology of the B^s gene will eventually grow to become a powerful tool in anthropological studies of Africans, and will complement archaeological and linguistic tools which have played significant roles in elucidating early African history, especially population migrations."[113] Adekile's prediction shows that sickling—now in the molecular biology form of the B^s gene—remains central to Western writing of Africa—past, present, and future.

Chapter 4
Sickling and the Paradoxes of African American Citizenship

In the late 1950s, sickling became increasingly well known—and increasingly fascinating—to the general public. In 1959, the *American Mercury*—a popular science magazine—carried an article on sickle cell anemia whose subtitle read "Tests for this little-known disease are important." Written by Lydia A. DeVilbiss, a physician, the article summarizes and simplifies—sometimes erroneously—the old physical anthropological discourse on blood and sickling which established both as race specific. It reads, among other things, as an indictment of the American Red Cross' policy (in effect since 1951) of not labeling blood in accordance with the race of the donor. Such a practice cannot be condoned, according to DeVilbiss, since "doctors who have had extensive experience in blood transfusions have given warning that the use of Negro blood in transfusions for white patients, and of white persons' blood for Negro patients, can result in unpleasant reactions."[1] I call attention to DeVilbiss's article here because in addition to expressing the racist concern that black people constitute a dysgenic threat to the social body, it establishes sickling as "an important health and economic problem" for "the Negro race,"[2] thus anticipating the discourses which in the 1970s were to make sickling, among other things, a public health issue and, consequently, a politicized disease.

Having made clear that a means exists for identifying those who unknowingly harbor the sickling trait and thus risk passing the burden of the debilitating disease on to their offspring, DeVilbiss suggests that the transmission of sickling be "managed" through mandatory premarital testing, just as venereal diseases have been "managed" through the required premarital Wassermann tests.[3] By linking the management of venereal disease (which is required by law) and that of sickling, DeVilbiss implies that both conditions fall within the realm of governance and must be addressed not only at the level of the individual sick body—in the clinic—but also at the level of the citizen, that is, through government programs and with respect to its implications for the society as a whole. If carriers of the sickle cell trait were identified and rendered visible, what was once a question of individual fate—if you were black you either got the disease or you did not, and you either passed it on or you did not—would be transformed into a matter of procreational choice based on risk assessment. By the same token, a means would be created for the governing of individual as well as familial conduct; what Donzelot has referred to as "government through the family."[4] The authorities could appeal to individuals armed with information about their inherited constitution to make socially responsible decisions—to invest not only in themselves but also in their families, their community, and their race.

For the first time in American discourse on sickling, then, the assumption emerges that the disease, which was seen as originating in the recesses of the "racial" (black) body, did not have to be met with resignation. For to recognize that it followed the Mendelian laws of inheritance and variability (that two carriers of the sickle cell trait had a one-in-four chance of having a child with the disease) was to acknowledge the possibility of managing it; that is, the possibility of transforming what was once the uncontrollable fate of race into a controllable genetic risk. In other words, DeVilbiss's article marks the beginning of the discursive transformation of sickling from a racial phenomenon into a genetic matter and, eventually, a matter of social administration.

In the 1970s this transformation gave political pertinence to the question of "control" and "prevention" in the governance of sickling. More specifically, in 1972, the U.S. Congress, in its first action on sickling, passed the National Sickle Cell Anemia *Control* Act. Following much alarm this legislation was retitled the National Sickle Cell Anemia *Prevention* Act. The substitution of "prevention" for "control" reflects the reformulation of the African American community, in the wake of the civil rights movement, from one that had to be acted upon to one capable of acting in its own interest. The discursive shift in emphasis from inheritance, racial ancestry, and adaptation to the role played by personal conduct and social formation in the containment or spread of a disease made possible the articulation of a strategy for the control and prevention of sickling.

I do not intend to suggest of course that sickling came under governance only in the 1970s. Prior to that time, the disease was governed, but strictly within medicine and anthropology. What happened in the 1970s was that the notion of "risk" with respect to sickling became tied to the black body in and of itself, whereas previously the risk in sickling was associated with interbreeding and articulated as a threat posed by black bodies to white bodies. Hence the urge of medicine at the time to police the boundaries between whites and blacks.

In this chapter I discuss what happened when control and prevention of sickling became much favored corrective measures of the welfare state, eager to make up for its long history of neglect of African Americans. Drawing upon the notion of government initially sketched out by Michel Foucault,[5] I delineate the shaping of civic power and identity emerging in the 1970s. More specifically, I show how an assemblage of tactics was informed by the notions of dreaded diseases of childhood, community, family, medicine, voluntary associations, and the neglected citizen, and how these tactics produced norms, procedures, and actions which molded African American identity and conduct so as to further certain political objectives on the part of both the state and an African American community that was newly enfranchised in the wake of the civil rights movement. I critically examine a number of non-clinical discourses on sickling, paying attention particularly to the transformations they underwent during the period in question. These transformations were a result of changes in the liberal discourse of and on governance, especially the growing importance attached to the notion that subjects of rule should be active participants in their own governance.[6]

Clearly, the achievement of full citizenship had been and remains a significant goal of African American engagement with United States government and legislation. In showing how the notion of government-sponsored sickle cell anemia control and prevention draws on and contributes to a discourse of African American citizenship, then, I am not arguing that the political goal of full citizenship was illegitimate, or that the practice of sickle cell anemia screening was ill advised or ill intentioned. I will demonstrate, however, the crucial reliance of the U.S. government's policy of prevention in the 1970s on a historically specific notion of personal responsibility, one that must be understood as neither ideologically transparent nor universally available to all political subjects. It is in part because the public and legislative discussion of what had been understood as a racial disease could now be used to demonstrate the government's changed stance toward African Americans that this policy became so heavily freighted with post–civil rights discourse of personal power, social responsibility, and full citizenship.

*   *   *

Following Michel Foucault, Nikolas Rose writes that government produces and is dependent upon two specific forms of knowledge about the population that is to be governed, isolation and inscription. On the one hand:

One needs to isolate it as a sector of reality, to identify certain characteristics and processes proper to it, to make its features notable, speakable, writable, to account for them according to certain explanatory schemes. Government thus depends upon the production, circulation, organization, and authorization of truths that incarnate what is to be governed, which make it thinkable, calculable, and practicable.[7]

On the other hand:

Governing a population requires knowledge of a different sort. To make calculations about a population necessitates the highlighting of certain features of that population as the raw material of calculation, and requires information about them. Knowledge here takes a very physical form; it requires the transcription of such phenomena as a birth, death . . . illness, the number of people living in this or that house . . . into material upon which political calculation can work. Calculation, that is to say, depends upon processes of "inscription", which translate the world into material traces: written reports, drawings, maps, charts.[8]

Rose's thesis valuably provides us with concrete guidelines for an analysis of the governance of sickling; for instance, it points to the importance of identifying the criteria used to differentiate sickling from other dreaded genetic diseases and to the need to account for the various strategies used to convince and mobilize black individuals and entire black communities to be tested for the sickle cell trait.

Whether the concern was to reduce the medico-genetic and economic consequences of sickling or to assign sickling the status of "dreaded disease of childhood" (which would influence private and public expenditures for treatment of and research on the disease), isolation and inscription were involved. Thus we might say that a study of the governance of sickling is akin to a survey of these two strategies of government.

In order to be governed, sickling had to be known; to be put into discourse; it had to be constituted as a distinct disease entity. Clearly, the 1970s did not bring sickling into discursive existence; it had a long and complex history, one that was dominated by the "anthropopathological" discourse on human breeding practices. Sickling was initially introduced into the fields of political argument and administrative practice as a means of defining the very traits that were perceived to characterize the Negro race, of regulating the relations between the races and of mapping the racial topography of various populations. However, in the 1970s, as the political debate came to be dominated by civil rights, the concept of race little by little became dissociated from biology and genetics and was rearticulated as a primarily socioeconomic phenomenon.

This may explain why, during this time, a political discourse on sickling—a black-related disease—could emerge, which, by emphasizing the social rather than the biogenetic dimensions of this well-documented phenomenon, successfully presented it as a new entity. As it (re)articulated the phenomenon as a means by which government could reach, regulate and redeem the African American population, this new sociopolitical discourse on sickling made of the disease a technology of governance. By presenting African Americans as people with the will and ability to act on their own behalf, it transformed African American subjectivity and agency into instruments of government.

*   *   *

I will begin this exploration of how sickling came to be seen as a potentially powerful vehicle of social transformation and reformation of "racial" relations by redrawing the most recent spaces of African American citizenship.

> [T]echnologies of the self (. . .) permit individuals to effect by their own means or with the help of others a certain number of operations on their own bodies and souls, thoughts, conduct, and way of being, so as to transform themselves in order to attain a certain state of happiness, purity, wisdom, perfection, or immortality.[9]

The management of sickling involved a sort of intensive care of the self and by extension of the race. Beginning in the late 1950s, continuing well into the 1970s, and with sporadic appearances in the 1980s, a new discourse on sickling could be heard articulating what might best be called a technology of the self. The fact that the medium of this discourse was circulated via popular magazines and newspapers has made some commentators notice that sickling at this point in time emerged from medical obscurity and gained general name recognition.[10] In the same year as the *American Mercury* carried its piece on blood and sickling, *Ebony* magazine — a monthly periodical widely read among the black middle class and featuring issues of concern to it — published the illness narrative of a twenty-one-year-old female college student with sickle cell anemia. The typical reader must have been a person who here, for the first time, was encountering the disease; that is to say, a person who had to come to terms with the information that it affects primarily — and commonly — the race to which he or she belongs and therefore is of more than mere theoretical relevance to him or her. Upon opening the magazine the reader comes face-to-face with a photograph of a young black woman; she appears physically debilitated; her facial expression is one of despair, a reflection, perhaps, of the disheartening consequences of a life lived with sickle cell anemia, a life depicted in the article as a series of unending battles with the disease. The headline reads, in bold type, "I'm Living on Borrowed Time":

> I have lived twenty-one years, two months, and seventeen days. Every minute of this time was "borrowed"; and by most medical standards I should have been dead long ago. But, through the goodness of God working through my parents, friends, dozens of doctors, nurses, and hundreds of blood donors, I still live. Over 250 pints of blood have been pumped into me in the last 21 years to sustain my life and, if I live my "three-score and ten" years, many times that number of blood transfusions will be necessary. Money was scarce in those days and the little that our family had

was swallowed up in doctor, medical, and hospital bills. Sometimes my hospital bill amounted to more during one week than my father earned the whole month. Most blood donors had to be paid, for many of them were college students, unskilled laborers, or men out of work who desperately needed twenty-five dollars to make ends meet. There were people who gave their blood free of charge, of course, and this group included church members, friends, strangers, and even nurses and doctors. My father gave several direct-line transfusions to me before he had to stop because he couldn't stand to lose more blood. Then he had to go searching for blood donors again.[11]

This excerpt first lays bare the impotence of clinical medicine in the face of sickling. Accompanying the text is a photograph of the patient standing behind (as if soon to be buried by) some 250 pints of empty blood bottles that she has allegedly been through. Those bottles of blood are all that medicine has to offer her; the medical workers can do no more than the layperson, we are told, namely donate their blood to the patient (as her own father has already done). The narrator owes her life, she states, not to medicine—"by most medical standards I should have been dead by now"—but to the "goodness of God" working through doctors and nurses in their capacity as blood donors as well as through her parents, her friends, and numerous other donors.

This passage also depicts the enormous physical and economic burden that the disease represents to the patient, as well as to her family, friends, strangers, and the medical care system. Sickling affects not only individual sick bodies—those suffering from sickle cell anemia—we learn, but an entire community or social body. The article makes clear that, while it may be a financial burden to those who have it, sickling also represents, in a very cruel fashion, an economic opportunity to those who live on the margins of the main economy—"college students, unskilled laborers, men out of work"—by creating a market for the very essence of their being, namely their blood. In the context of sickling, according to the article, medicine has failed, and to those affected by the disease survival means a slow and painful death.

Just as important, this narrative creates a space for the sick person's subjective, internal, or psychological experience of her disease—a space that does not exist in earlier, mainly biomedical accounts of sickling—by bringing into the picture such notions as temptation, stubbornness, perseverance, and feeling sorry for one-self:

Many times there was a strong temptation to withdraw from college, go home, climb into bed, and stay there until I rusted away. But I never did. It was stubbornness rather than mere perseverance, that kept me going from day to day. When I finally stopped feeling sorry for myself and looked around me I saw how blessed I was. A friend of mine, who was about my age and was my roommate several times in St. Mary's Hospital, had been ill all her life, too. Because I was so wrapped up in my own problems, it took me a long time to realize that she was in the hospital when I came, while I was there, and was still there after I left. . . . What right had I to feel sorry for myself? I spent the majority of my time out of the hospital.[12]

The excerpt cited above represents coping with sickling mainly as an attitudinal challenge and relates the narrator's successful at-tempt at applying what Foucault calls a technology of the self, that is to say, at transforming her own thoughts (attitude) to obtain, in this case, what is described as a state of bliss—"When I finally stopped feeling sorry for myself and looked around me, I saw how blessed I was." The narrator is concerned with the ways in which she can change herself, not with the ways in which she could act on her broader medicosocial context.

Seven years after the publication of "I'm Living on Borrowed Time," *Ebony* magazine returned to the subject of sickling, this time with an article entitled "Incurable 'Negro Disease' Strikes Five In Family." Consider first the problem of visualization and cognition. Beside the title, listed above, is a picture of a standard middle-class split-level house; the blinds are closed; on the front door is a sign on which is faintly written "for sale." In the context suggested by the title, namely incurable disease, this picture of a house en-veloped in darkness by closed shutters and with a sign on the door evokes the nineteenth-century sanitary practice of evacuating and boarding up houses inhabited by people with contagious diseases and affixing a "sick: caution" sign on the door. A link is estab-lished, in other words, between a genetic disease—sickling—and dreaded communicable diseases such as tuberculosis. Paradoxi-cally, the text explicitly refutes this connection: "The whole family shares a sense of loneliness and separation from the community, for some people mistakenly believe sickle cell anemia is something that can be caught like a cold."[13] This paradox is worth noticing because the congressional debates on sickling in the 1970s were complicated precisely by the fact that they were caught in the tension between the unfounded but deep-seated fear of transmission through casual contact and the well-documented fact that sickling is a genetic disease which can be passed on but not caught.

This narrative is pertinent here, however, because it represents the emerging discourse on prevention through intervention at the level of procreative practices:

> The only preventative means possible is to avoid the mating of people who both have the sickle cell trait for, according to the mechanics of heredity, it would be likely that at least one-fourth of their children would develop the actual disease . . . Sickle cell trait, or the carrier state, can be detected by simple and inexpensive tests which can be administered at a hospital or clinic. Many of those who are aware that they have the disease or trait have taken it into consideration when choosing a mate, some going so far as to be willing to give up the loved one if any evidence of sickling is revealed in premarital tests.[14]

This passage suggests that the solution to matters that we have come to view as highly personal ones (such as the choice of a mate) may be incompatible with our responsibilities as members of a family or community. Unlike the account quoted earlier, which depicted medicine's impotence in the face of sickling and presented intervention as being possible only at the level of the self and in the form of a change of attitude, this article outlines a plan for action at the interpersonal level. More specifically, it indicates a strategy of prevention—testing for the sickle cell trait and modification of the procreational conduct of carriers of the trait. Although this strategy is to be applied by individuals, it is not meant to improve conditions within the sphere of the self, but rather to positively affect entire families and communities. By emphasizing that some people have already let their social responsibilities take precedence over the satisfaction of their personal desires—"Some going so far as to be willing to give up the loved one if any evidence of sickling is revealed in premarital tests"—the article implicitly endorses the notions of the "informed (procreational) choice" and the socially responsible individual.

That sickling is a black-related disease was presumed to be a matter of fact in most personal sickling narratives. However, the narratives articulated "blackness" as a principle of alliance rather than a biogenetic or racial matter. The locus of the disease was the black community, and the body at risk—the target of intervention—was the black social body.

The personal sickling narratives are what Rose calls "inscriptive devices" in that they were instrumental in a specific form of subject formation which, in this case, was organized around the idea of personal responsibility.[15] In the 1970s, the conduct of individuals with sickling in the context of procreation became an administrative matter, a site of governmental intervention and regulation. As the notion of personal responsibility was the means by which government exercised its control, the personal conduct of those targeted by the various government programs to control and prevent sickling, namely African Americans, became a fundamentally public and political matter rather than a private and moral one. The sickling narratives articulated what was to become the new political subjectivity of African Americans.[16]

Personal responsibility as a technology of the self had long been a strategy of governance favored by modern liberal democratic states. The specific way this notion was used in discussions of sickle cell anemia in the 1970s had to do with the historical conjunction of this strategy with emerging and newly successful demands for enfranchisement on the part of African Americans. Because this new governmental policy of prevention required acknowledgment of a history of neglect of the disease—which at least implicitly admitted the government's role in maintaining racism—sickle cell anemia prevention provided the government with the opportunity to answer African American demands for reparation and full citizenship. Yet, because the government's deployment of the category of personal responsibility was ultimately always in the service of its own hierarchies and necessary exclusions, the new policy also created an expanded opportunity for governmental scrutiny and control of African American communities. It is this contradiction to which African American critics of the policy were to respond.

*   *   *

While the sickling narratives brought the disease to the attention of the black middle class, it remained largely unknown to the less affluent segments of the black population and to the general

American public. This state of affairs was documented by J. C. Lane and Robert B. Scott who found that only three out of ten African American adults in Richmond, Virginia, had heard of sickle cell anemia.[17] A year later, Scott published a set of statistics on the so-called dreaded diseases of childhood detailing for each disease the incidence, the sources of funding for and the amount of money spent on testing, treatment and research, and public awareness.[18] These statistics identified sickling as "a community health problem," a finding that would have profound consequences insofar as it labeled sickling as a matter requiring government intervention and situated the disease in an intricate network of political and medical rationalities.

In addressing sickling, according to Scott, priority had to be given to the creation of public awareness—of the disease and of the need for financial support. The defining characteristic of the discourse that Scott epitomized was, as we shall see, the emphasis that it put on the redistribution of health care resources. It was crucial, in Scott's view, to know how sickling compared with related ailments, such as childhood and ethnic diseases. Viewing sickling as a childhood disease, Scott found that while sickling outpaced many comparable diseases in relative incidence and severity, it lagged significantly behind them in public and private funds received for basic research and clinical investigation:

In 1967 there were an estimated 1,155 new cases of SCA [sickle cell anemia], 1,206 of cystic fibrosis, 813 of muscular dystrophy, and 350 of phenylketonuria. Yet volunteer organizations raised $1.9 million for cystic fibrosis, $7.9 million for muscular dystrophy, but less than $100,000 for SCA. National Institutes of Health grants for many less common hereditary illnesses exceed those for SCA.[19]

This led Scott to ask: "What priority does this problem deserve and what priority does it presently receive in the distribution of healthcare resources?" However, in trying to answer this question, Scott did not go beyond the questions of severity and prevalence—the measures on which he differentiated sickling from other childhood diseases, and on which he would argue for the reprioritization of funding resources.[20]

While Scott made clear the disparity in funding of the various childhood diseases, he did not critically examine the reasons for this disparity, conditions which, as we shall see, are not always medical. Scott showed that financial support from public and private sources for all the "important" childhood diseases (diabetes mellitus, acute leukemia, cystic fibrosis, muscular dystrophy, and phenylketonuria) far outpaced sickling, despite the fact that the latter's incidence was five times the rate of its closest rival. In an attempt to pinpoint the cause of this state of affairs, he compared sickling to other diseases and found that sickling lacked the public relations apparatus so crucial in rendering visible and furthering fundraising for and awareness of diseases like cystic fibrosis and muscular dystrophy. "First, there are no nationwide volunteer organizations devoted to sickle cell anemia. [While] nationwide volunteer organizations involved in cystic fibrosis and muscular dystrophy are quite prominent and effective." [21]

Scott's explanation of and implicit solution to the neglect of sickling has been met with little opposition. However, I would like to push his analysis further by looking more closely at the phenomena with which the disease is being compared. Scott did not problematize the public image of cystic fibrosis, muscular dystrophy, and cerebral palsy. But a careful examination shows these phenomena to be meticulously scripted entities, owing their visibility to—as Scott rightly points out—an enormous public relations bureaucracy. This bureaucracy makes these diseases and the persons suffering from them visible to society by parading them before the nation every year, usually as part of a fundraising campaign. (One thinks here of "Jerry's Kids" on comedian Jerry Lewis's long-running annual telethon for muscular dystrophy.) A characteristic feature of the public relations efforts on behalf of these diseases and those who are affected by them is their insistence on the emotional as well as the medical dimensions of disease and patienthood. While they represent the diseases as medical categories (pathologies in need of a cure), they also sentimentalize them (much is made, for instance, of the innocence of the victims—who are often children—and of the unjust nature of their predicament). Those having the diseases are granted a special sort of second-class "disease citizenship," namely that of "cripples," on the grounds that their disorders make it impossible for them to meet the requirements for full citizenship. [22]

Following Scott's unearthing of the disparity in public awareness and financial support between sickling and other diseases of childhood, some African Americans sought to increase funding for sickling research by turning to telethons, modeled on those for cystic fibrosis, muscular dystrophy, and cerebral palsy. These telethons were unsuccessful not because of the clinical nature of sickling, but because they were unable to neutralize the historical difference of the population in which sickling was primarily found—African Americans.[23] (Such a neutralization would have required making a nonissue of the discrimination to which the latter have historically been subject.) This in turn made it impossible to sentimentalize sickling in accordance with the model for disease representation required by the genre of the telethon.

Sickling was, for Scott, more than anything else a social issue, specifically, an important public health issue of the urban sphere:

Where to place the emphasis for the most effective use of funds and efforts is another important question. Since the majority of Negroes now live in urban areas, sickle cell anemia becomes a major health consideration for those involved in community health in the cities. In cities with sizeable Negro populations, sickle cell anemia is not just another significant health problem but one of the more prevalent health problems.[24]

"Urban areas"—understood as cities with sizable Negro populations—became a key term in the emerging discussions on sickling as a public health problem as well as in the hygienic discourse on sickling prevention. Sickling was presented not only as a flaw within the constitution of the black body, but also, more important, as a particular threat to urban black communities. By articulating sickling as a problem affecting certain communities and places rather than isolated individuals—as a condition aggravated by the very nature of urban living—Scott implicitly made key issues of "hygiene" (understood as the rules of conduct individuals must follow for their own bodies in order to protect the overall social body) as well as government neglect. The term "urban area" came to designate the space where medicine and politics converged.

"Governing" sickling thus defined via hygienic prevention policies presupposed the existence of a community whose members were ready, willing, and able to make effective use of information. Whether the black community had these characteristics was at the time a subject of debate. Beginning in the 1960s and throughout the 1970s, a variety of individuals and institutions began to express concern about the condition of the black community: educators, family experts, the police, the courts, social workers, doctors, and community activists.

Moynihan's Report of 1965—*The Negro Family: The Case for National Action*—summarizes (for President Lyndon B. Johnson) what was perceived to be the problem.[25] The report, which was intended as a proposal for social policy, linked the failure of the black community to achieve middle-class status to such phenomena as broken families, illegitimacy, matriarchy, welfare dependency, delinquency, and crime. The representation of the black family as dysfunctional was a product of specific dominant discourses on "the family" and rendered possible—and justified—certain strategies of intervention.

The picture of the African American community that the Moynihan Report drew was in stark contrast to that suggested by Scott: "Today young people are learning principles of heredity in high school," he says, "and family planning has become acceptable and more effective. Lack of awareness of the illness [sickling] is a lesser problem to solve today because of the effectiveness of educational and communication media."[26] The principles of heredity were part of the high school curriculum of the day. However, given the nature of Scott's project, one is struck by his uncritical representation of the schools and the media as the sole determining factors in creating a successful sickle cell anemia prevention program. Conspicuously, Scott fails to engage the widely disseminated view of the black community as dysfunctional at the level of the family as well as at the level of the community itself, the view summarized by the Moynihan Report. That is not to say that the report was right; I am simply calling attention to the fact that the report represented the dominant discourse on the black community at the time, a fact which makes Scott's silence on it the more remarkable.

Scott moves on to make a case for genetic testing for the sickle cell trait:

The most important factor which would make a preventive program effective would be the early knowledge of trait-carrying. If screening were offered prior to marriage age, those who were found to carry an abnormal gene could be counselled to be sure that their mates were tested at the time of marriage. Only in this way, can heterozygote pairs . . . be detected and only in this way can informed decisions be made about childbearing among parents at risk. . . . Whether a young couple will decide to have no children or plan a limited family size or disregard the knowledge of the risk would be entirely their own decision. . . . However, the opportunity to protect their families from the tragedy of sickle cell anemia has not been offered. . . . It is not only because of its neglect that sickle cell anemia deserves higher priority. . . . This may be the first hereditary illness which could be controlled by genetic counselling.[27]

While the personal sickling narratives from *Ebony* examined earlier were about individuals and their families struggling privately to manage the disease, Scott's work shows that the personal or private is inescapably political. Thus, it takes sickling well beyond the realms of the sick person and clinical medicine, into the domain of public health and its surveillance strategies. This move coincides with the substitution of the trait for the anemia as the site of intervention. What needs to be acted upon, according to Scott, is not the anemia or sick bodies but the spaces between bodies where the trait is being passed on through mating. It is, in other words, the conduct of the healthy—those referred to by *Ebony* magazine as "the countless couples to whom . . . knowledge came too late"— that the state must seek to govern.[28]

The trait (and not the anemia) would ultimately provide a site for the surveillance of the reproductive behavior of African Americans. More precisely, it became the vehicle for the constitution of the particular type of African American subjects who armed with knowledge—thanks to "the effectiveness of the educational and communication media today," as Scott would have it—made informed decisions. These subjects, supposedly unlike previous generations of African Americans, fulfilled the requirements for full citizenship and possessed knowledge of what they needed to do in order to serve their own interest and that of their community, and to act accordingly.

Power as embedded in the technology of genetic testing and in the notion of the benefits of screening for the sickle cell trait is noncoercive. It does not will itself onto the subject; rather, it works—discursively—by formulating a specific kind of subjectivity for those defined as the "beneficiaries" of the screening practice. Because the prevention of sickling could not be successful without the active (that is, informed) participation of the black community, that population had to be rendered as receptive to information and as capable of acting on its own behalf. This was effected by Scott's spelling out the competence of young (black) people at the time. The government—in insisting on the need to "inform" African Americans—was not responding to a matter of fact, namely the "ignorance" of the latter, but rather, in order to be able to govern at all, the government inscribed African Americans with features that it could then act upon.

I have privileged Scott's text because I view it as foundational insofar as it summarizes the various discourses and practices that were to shape the governance of sickling in the 1970s. By showing that sickling—presumably a black-related disease—had clearly been abandoned by private and public charities, Scott's article turned the disease into an appropriate site for reparational government intervention on behalf of African Americans. Specifically, it made possible the articulation of a discourse on sickling organized around the notion of government neglect. This constituted the medical relation to sickling in the 1970s, not unlike the way that race in its biologizing form came to construct sickling in the 1930s. This discourse, in turn, made possible the contention that there was such a thing as one unified black community, namely a community whose members were joined by their collective experience of marginality with respect to government. In the wake of Scott's work, the government sought to remedy past "oversights" by encouraging the black community to take an active part in being screened for the sickle cell trait and in obtaining counseling about the risk of having a child with sickle cell anemia. In return for black engagement, the government established and funded the programs needed to reinforce the transformation of African Americans into active, responsible, and productive citizens. By isolating the black community as a target of governance and calculating and inscribing its competence, Scott's work laid the groundwork for the government's policy of action.

*   *   *

The following call for action at all levels of society in the war on sickling is an excerpt from the editorial accompanying Scott's report in the *Journal of the American Medical Association*:

It is difficult to overstate the need for action at local, state, and national levels. . . . Sickle cell anemia is one of the most common long-term illnesses of black children. The economic implications are staggering. Victims of the disease encounter employee rejection, insurance rejection, and high medical costs. At a time when airlines, for instance, are expanding job opportunities for blacks, many qualified applicants are being turned away because they are carriers of sickle cell anemia. . . . The facts are clear. Hopefully, the clarion call has been sounded for action. New neighborhood health centers are being developed in many areas where there is a high density of black citizens. There is no better place to begin the translation of what is known about sickle cell anemia into beneficial community programs.[29]

This passage outlines the political and economic problems posed by sickling and the gains that could be derived from the management of the disease. It is organized around three major themes: first, the economic burden the disease represents to the sick person and his or her family who are commonly impoverished by the cost of blood transfusions and other treatment; second, sickling in the context of discrimination and rights in employment and insurance; third, sickling as an ultimately "beneficial scourge" for the black community in that its management encourages the ongoing process of establishing neighborhood health centers in areas with a high density of black citizens.

The text is not explicit about what is known about sickle cell anemia and what beneficial community programs might be gleaned from it, but both are important for understanding what follows. First, what was known about sickling was its mode of inheritance and, consequently, the means for its prevention. Second, the community health centers that were being created in black neighborhoods were also appropriate and convenient sites for screening for sickling. As these centers trained and employed a host of local people as health care workers, they—and by extension the governance of sickling—became linked to another effort, "the war on poverty," especially to the revitalization of the poor black urban communities.

The rearticulation of sickling—in a medical journal—through the socioeconomic discourse of policy making is characteristic of the reformulation of the relationship between medicine and politics which took place in the 1970s. President Nixon's 1971 State of the Union message epitomizes this fusion of the medical and the political in the context of sickling:

It is a sad and shameful fact that the cause of this disease [sickling] has been largely neglected throughout our history. We cannot rewrite this record of neglect, but we can reverse it.[30]

In this remorseful statement Nixon explicitly admits that government has historically failed to address the cause of sickling; he also implicitly acknowledges that, consequently, those who were commonly known to be the most affected by the disease—African Americans—have been subject of government neglect and have effectively been relegated to the status of second-class citizens. However, when declaring that government's "record of neglect" with respect to sickling can be reversed, Nixon implies that government's neglect of African Americans *can* be reversed, that government could conceivably take responsibility for the well-being of African Americans, thus integrating them into the civic body as full citizens. In this respect, his statement acknowledges the possibility of making a new black citizen body through the governance of sickling.

Immediately after Nixon's address, the Senate Subcommittee on Health initiated hearings on sickling, (November 11 and 12, 1971) intending to enact what was initially referred to as the National Sickle Cell Anemia Control Act. The term "control" was quickly replaced by the term "prevention" when activists within the black community pointed to the unfortunate connotations of the former term. Diseases requiring "control" are communicable diseases, and that was exactly what sickle cell anemia was not. One of the main goals of those engaged in the sickle cell debate was to eradicate the myth that sickling could be contracted like the common cold. To make clear to the general public that sickling was not a contagious disease to be controlled but a genetic disorder to be prevented would eliminate, it seemed, the stigmatization of the black population through sickling.

The hearings were attended by a wide variety of people. Politicians and policy makers, community activists, private citizens, and representatives of voluntary associations (American Nurses Association, National Urban League, Inc., NAACP, Sickle Cell Disease Research Foundation of California, etc.) all seized on sickling as a means of transforming the black community, including rearticulating its relationship with government. Ambitiously, the participants in the hearings viewed sickling as a vehicle for reconfiguring the responsibilities of the state toward African Americans, more specifically, as a means of reformulating black citizenship, and thereby, the boundaries of civil society.

"Neglect" became a key word in the hearings, and the powerful emotional appeal of that term may have made the hearings so effective in seizing the imagination of politicians, policy makers, and ordinary people alike. The participants in the hearings called on the state to recognize that neglect (embodied now in sickling) was a defining feature of the African American experience, and presented the governance of sickling as a potentially powerful corrective measure.

Another recurrent term throughout the hearings was "the black community." However, rather than assuming that the black community existed in some essential and representable form prior to the hearings, I would like to show that the hearings resulted in a particular articulation of the black community, which was an entity subject to change rather than an invariable matter of fact. In other words, I view the hearings—like the personal sickling narratives mentioned earlier—not just as a forum where the views of a preexisting, unified black community could be represented by experts, government witnesses, and common people (as an instance of the governance of opinion), but rather as a device for inscribing a certain community. Out of the cacophony of voices testifying about the neglect of the black population, and identifying the means by which the latter could be corrected, emerged a discursive assemblage—the black community. The hearings, thus, represented the isolation of the black population as an object of governance; they identified the capacities (the productive potential of its internal organization) and deficiencies of the latter; and they inscribed these capacities and deficiencies in a policy—prevention through screening—aimed at preserving and protecting the health and welfare of all citizens.

The hearings concluded with the enactment of the National Sickle Cell Anemia Prevention Act. In this document, Congress outlined what it had come to perceive—as a result of the hearings—as the relevant facts about sickling as well as its own objectives:

(1) that sickle cell anemia is a disease resulting from the inheritance of a genetic factor relating to the sickle cell trait which afflicts a large number of American citizens, primarily among the black population . . . ;
(2) that the disease is a deadly and tragic burden which strikes approximately one of every five hundred black children, and

less than half of those children who contract the disease sur-
vive beyond the age of twenty;

(3) that efforts to prevent sickle cell anemia must be directed
towards increased research in the cause and treatment of the
disease, and the education, screening and counseling of carriers of the sickle cell trait;

(4) that simple and inexpensive screening tests have been de-
vised which will identify those who have the disease or carry
the trait;

(5) that programs to control sickle cell anemia must be based
entirely upon the voluntary cooperation of the individual involved;

(6) that the attainment of better methods of control, diagnosis,
and treatment of sickle cell anemia deserves the highest priority.[31]

The Act, while addressing a genetic disease, also represented
the discursive construction of a black citizen body: it outlined the
explanation of and solution to sickling, and the means whereby
this solution could be effected. According to the Act, sickling is an
inherited disease afflicting a large number of American citizens,
constituting a "tragic burden," particularly to the black population.
The problem to be addressed was defined as sickle cell anemia,
and priority was given to a certain strategy of preventive intervention, namely (genetic) screening in conjunction with education
and counseling. This strategy seemed all the more attractive because the technical means for identifying those who carried within
them the potentially deadly trait (inexpensive screening tests) were
already available. The Act concluded with a statement of purpose:
"to preserve and protect the health and welfare of all citizens." In
articulating its ultimate goal in this way, Congress reaffirmed the
basic obligation of the liberal democratic state toward all of its
members, thus, in principle, conferring full citizenship to African
Americans.

As one would expect, the prevention policy addressed the trait—
not the anemia (the actual disease). Whereas the anemia was seen
at the time as falling unquestionably within the domain of medicine, the trait was never successfully medicalized, despite many
attempts. The trait historically had existed somewhere in between

the medical and the social, and it was this terrain that the hearings and the Act were remapping (see Chapters 1 and 2).

Throughout the hearings numerous inaccurate statements were made about the incidence of the trait, the relationship between the trait and the anemia, and the nature of the anemia. (These inaccuracies were not specific to the discourse on sickling articulated in the hearings, but were commonly found in the various public discourses on the phenomenon circulating in the media.) For example, the anemia rate was repeatedly said to be higher than it was, in many instances because it was confused with the trait. This error is worth noticing because it helped create the sense of urgency that permeated the hearings. By presenting a genetic phenomenon affecting a fraction of the black population as a crisis of the black population in general, the participants in the hearings paradoxically failed to dissociate themselves from the contagious disease model through which the black body has been understood since the nineteenth century.[32] Sickling as represented in the hearings put the entire black population at risk. The sense of alarm was intensified by the fact that the anemia was consistently depicted as signifying imminent death, remarks being made again and again about those with the disease dying before the age of twenty.

In this respect, the hearings constituted yet another of the many inscriptive devices which in the 1970s rendered the black community as one characterized by its state of crisis and need of immediate government intervention. (The Moynihan Report was another such device.) This inscription of the black community was carried out, on the one hand, through a dramatization of sickling's medico-social aspects and the government's failure to adequately address these aspects, and, on the other hand, through the insistence on the notion of urgency. Immediate action was widely represented by senators, congressional representatives, and those providing testimony as the means through which the government could show its willingness to fulfill its responsibilities toward black Americans.

However, the hearings made clear that government was not a unified body. Authorities from the National Institutes of Health (NIH) called for a more cautionary approach to the black community and the disease. In an exchange between the chairman, Senator Edward M. Kennedy (D.-Mass.), and Doctors Frank Beckles and John Zapp from NIH, the latter pointed to the lack of an appropriate infrastructure (trained counselors, facilities, and equipment) for dealing with the problems that a mass screening program would entail and suggested that a more gradual approach be considered.[33] Senator Kennedy, however, was intent on "acting immediately." His eagerness to establish a screening program without delay can be gleaned from his rather impatient interrogation of the doctors: "What is the best way to meet that quandary; is it not to have a program or to have a program? . . . Just answer."[34] In pointing to Kennedy's zealous insistence on immediate action as opposed to the doctors' call for caution and further preparation, I do not wish to call into question the genuineness of the concern for the well-being of individuals with sickle cell anemia or the sense of social justice that suffused both approaches. My aim is simply to show that the category of immediacy in the context of the hearings, far from being ideologically transparent, was charged with political signification.

However far apart Beckles and Zapp (from the NIH), Kennedy (and the Congress), and the various participants at-large (representing a number of private and very diverse constituencies) may seem, they were in agreement on two crucial issues: (1) sickling—and blacks—had historically been neglected by the government, and (2) genetic screening was the appropriate strategy to use in order to reduce the incidence of sickling and redeem the black population. Beckles and Zapp were not representing the position of Nixon's Administration, which less than a year earlier had brought the major social programs enacted in the 1960s—the War on Poverty—to a halt, vetoing over $2 billion of legislative programs for education and health care for children of low-income families, including Head Start. The Nixon Administration was clearly more inclined to address the government's neglect of specific segments of the population through genetic screening—a relatively inexpensive strategy—than to work to transform the social and racial hierarchies that produced the neglect in the first place.

As the government set out to protect the health and welfare of the black community, it utilized the social infrastructure of that community. This strategy was deemed necessary because the success of the sickling prevention program was perceived to depend upon the extent of voluntary cooperation from African Americans. This in turn required that African Americans be made to see screening as something they needed and would benefit from. Education therefore had to be an integral part of the sickling prevention program. Information about the disorder needed to be made part of the grade school curriculum and the professional medical training. It had to be made available in shopping centers, at neighborhood clinics, at fairs, in churches, at the work place, and other locations. Through this massive educational effort, the government would seek to turn the black community into a site of medico-social administration and individual blacks into sentries of the overall population in order to prevent the passing of a lethal trait to the next generation.

A policy statement on health, "Toward a National Health Program," submitted by the National Urban League during the hearings, called for the deployment within the black community of a whole cadre of paraprofessionals recruited from within that very community. Of relevance is the following passage from the statement:

Faced with impossible shortages of care-giving personnel, institutions all over the nation are finding new avenues of more effective service in the "paraprofessional," the warm, emphathetic person who not only relates more easily and more personally to the patient in distress but who also carries a significant and substantial part of the work load previously reserved for professionals. . . . In less than a week . . . hospitals . . . have trained aides, most of whom are black and not formally educated beyond ninth grade, to take and record temperatures and blood pressures, routines that at one time were thought to require a full nursing education. . . . Not long ago the U.S. Army began to produce "social work/psychology specialists" in a ten week training program. Needless to say, the enlisted men often find these "specialists" easier to talk to and confide in than the Army psychiatrist. . . . Similar situations prevail in civilian life, especially in rural or disadvantaged urban communities where differences in status or race tend to act as barriers to communication between the highly trained, middle class professional and the patient in need of his services. In such instances, the use of the paraprofessional aides may be essential to the delivery and maintenance of high quality, dignified and comprehensive care.[35]

In the sickling prevention program set out by the National Sickle Cell Anemia Prevention Act, paraprofessionals were to be linked to the machinery of government at certain points: at centers of research and service, in screening and education clinics, and in the offices of local doctors. This would allow the government to intervene at a distance, taking action—or exercising its power—while remaining relatively unobtrusive.

The willingness of the black community to accept intervention on a massive scale was an explicitly stated concern throughout the hearings. Very early on Senators Kennedy and John V. Tunney (D-Calif.) spoke directly to this matter in an exchange regarding the content of the bill the latter cosigned:

Senator Edward Kennedy: But do you agree with me that many black people would like to be tested if they had the facilities to go to some place where this service was available to them?
Senator Tunney: That is true. I think it is absolutely true.
Senator Kennedy: As a matter of fact, the leadership has really been provided by the Black Athletes Foundation, Dr. Scott of Howard University and, many other groups in this area. They have challenged the Congress to take some kind of meaningful action, and I think your bill does just that.[36]

Later in the hearings Kennedy posed a similar question to Representative William Clay—a Congressman from Missouri:

Senator Edward Kennedy: I was interested, Congressman, are there any voluntary programs in your district in Missouri, efforts that are being made to develop programs or screening programs?
Congressman William Clay: Well, there are a few efforts in the St. Louis area that we are attempting to get off the ground. One of the problems is that we do not have the capacity for raising the kind of money that is necessary. There are some dedicated people in my area but they do not have the resources. There are some people who are attempting to counsel and test those who may have the trait; but other than that, there is no effective kind of program in my community or in any others, to my knowledge. . . .
Senator Edward Kennedy: . . . And I think that what you are expressing is representative of the people of your community as well as many other communities, that there is a desire of the people to have it done and there are existing facilities in various communities, I think. There is a will and desire for this kind of program. You have mentioned the voluntary efforts that are getting off the

ground in your community and we are hearing examples of this in practically every community across the country.[37]

These passages show that knowing the will of the black community and documenting the community's willingness to help itself and to lead the effort were central concerns. Self-governance was the goal, and as a consequence those invited to represent the community were queried continuously about its internal workings. Senator Kennedy did not leave the matter with Congressman William Clay, but raised it again with Dr. Elmer Anderson and Dr. Accie Mitchell, chairman and board member of the Research Foundation for Sickle Cell Anemia in Los Angeles—who were presented as "ethnographers" with a firsthand knowledge of the black community:

Senator Edward Kennedy: And do you know as a doctor whether there are people who would be willing to be trained to give these tests? Are there members of either the black or white community that are prepared to be trained to help administer the test?
Dr. Elmer Anderson: Yes, sir. We think there would be a lot of people. . . .
Dr. Accie Mitchell: The main problem that we have out in the Los Angeles area in the ghetto is the fact that we do not have the money to test these people. It is simply because of the fact that there are no funds available. We have the personnel and we have the doctor volunteers who are willing to go out and see that these tests are done and carried out properly, but as long as we do not have any money we run into a problem of calling off tests; and then people become dissatisfied with the way we are conducting the tests . . . ; they cannot be tested when they want to be tested, and therefore the cause becomes a little bit unpopular and we lose a lot of people that we could have found. . . .
Senator Edward Kennedy: What is the willingness of the members of the community to take these tests? Do you find that there is an interest in it? Are they willing to take these tests if it is given at a decent time and under adequate kinds of circumstances and in clean facilities? . . . As people who have worked in this field, Doctor, for some 13 years; are people willing to be tested? Do they want to know about sickle cell anemia?

Dr. Elmer Anderson: Very much so. We had one example. We had what we called "Sickle Cell Month" during the month of September. On one occasion, just one of our neighborhood newspapers had a note that there would be a clinic testing, and I think on one day we had to turn away something like 250 people. . . . Senator Kennedy, I have also heard some feedback on this, that people are afraid that if you tell them what they have you are going to create hysteria.

Senator Edward Kennedy: We heard that yesterday [Reference here is to Dr. Frank Beckles's testimony].

Dr. Elmer Anderson: I think that is the most asinine kind of thing . . . , it is like the young woman who comes in with a lump in her breast —she might be frightened, but she wants to know what it is. I think this is how most of the black people feel who are aware of the fact that health is an important factor.

Senator Edward Kennedy: Do I interpret your comment that if we were to provide what I think is an extremely small amount of resources for the development of an educational, screening, and testing program, that people would take advantage of it and welcome it in terms of your experience in working in this field for 13 years, rather than being frightened by it?

Dr. Elmer Anderson: That is my opinion; yes, sir. They would take advantage of it and be very, very thankful and happy to have it. We think that we owe this to our citizenry.[38]

I will conclude by citing comments made by representatives of the Black Athletes Foundation—Horace Davis, the executive director, who was accompanied by John Henry Johnson, Henry ("Hank") Aaron, and Dr. Anthony J. Giorgio. The presence of the foundation at the hearings was deemed important because of its high public visibility and leadership role and because of the program on sickling it had enacted in the Pittsburgh area. Once again, Senator Kennedy led the questioning:

Senator Edward Kennedy: Is it your (Aaron—for the Black Athletes Foundation) impression from your contacts with thousands of people that they would welcome this kind of a program to provide some screening and testing and education in terms of the nature of the disease?

Mr. Henry Aaron: I think this is the only way that it could probably be stamped out, and I think that the people that I have talked to welcome a program of this sort.

Senator Edward Kennedy: Now, it has been suggested . . . that if you pass this kind of legislation . . . you are going to frighten members of the black community and perhaps others as well because of the enormity of the program, and you are going to stir things up and make them scared. What is your reaction and feeling about this? Do you think that is true or do you think people would welcome this kind of help and assistance?

Mr. Henry Aaron: I think they would welcome it, really.

Senator Edward Kennedy: How committed is the foundation, at least, to trying to address themselves to this problem? How strongly do they really care about it? How firmly are they committed to it?

Dr. Anthony J. Giorgio: . . . The Black Athletes Foundation's greatest asset is their obvious ability to increase the awareness among the black population of this society. . . . Mr. Davis and the Black Athletes Foundation approached us who are members of the Department of Medicine at the University of Pittsburgh in the Hematology Section, and they asked us for some help . . . for a screening program which [they] . . . might hold in an East Hill shopping center outside of central Pittsburgh; and [they] assured me that [they] could attract 4,000 or 5,000 black people for screening. . . . I doubted it because we had attempted mass screening programs and the most people we ever screened happened to be 800. As it turned out, 5,000 people showed up at this activity, about 99.9 percent of whom were black, all for sickle cell screening. Because we ran out of supplies, we screened just slightly less than 4,000 in 3 days.

Senator Kennedy: The limitation, then, was really on the adequacy of the resources, because of financial support; is that right?

Dr. Anthony J. Giorgio: Yes.[39]

By repeatedly checking the community's willingness to act on its own behalf, to offer itself up for screening, the Senate was responding to a concern raised not by the black community but by government itself. This concern was conditioned in part by an earlier (and, at the time of the hearings, still ongoing) debate on family planning which some had seen as defining blacks as a target of population control. This debate had led to cries of genocide from within certain segments of the black community and had put the government in the position of the perpetrator and made of it an institution not to be trusted.[40]

In the context of sickling, therefore, the government wanted to be seen as responding to needs defined by the black community itself. The government was in a precarious situation, however. Having openly acknowledged its complicity in the neglect of sickling and African Americans (Nixon's State of the Union message), it was forced — by public opinion — to take action, yet it had to avoid being seen as acting unilaterally. Rather than imposing a screening program on the black population, running the risk of being accused of ignoring the will of those to be screened, the government had to solicit and ensure the active participation of the black community. Most important, it had to be clear that the government was following the lead of the people, not the other way round. Kennedy went so far as to present the government as slowing down the implementation of a much needed sickling prevention program. In his words, the black community was well ahead on the matter:

It is clear that the American people want this kind of program. If we are going to begin to insure that this Government is responsive, we must adopt this kind of program. . . . Would you (Senator Brooke) not agree with me that this has been one instance where the people have been ahead of the Government; they have been pleading for this kind of program in the field, and that we must really meet our responsibility by accepting the challenge to move ahead in this critical area of health need?[41]

The statement "[o]ne instance where the people have been ahead of the Government," though seemingly innocuous, is worth scrutinizing if only for the centrality it affords the notion of "the people" (read "the black community"!).[42] It clearly suggests a desire for a more inclusive policy toward African Americans, in that it refers to the American people rather than singling out the black population. In this respect it represents an implicit articulation of African Americans as democratic subjects ready to tackle the problems with which they are faced. It can also be read as a (counter)-discourse on the black community in that it formulates the latter as a well-organized and well-informed community (along the lines of Scott's work). Such a version of the black community is a far cry from the dysfunctional and irresponsible population described in the Moynihan Report. Most important, the statement makes clear that the people is "pleading" for government responsiveness and action.

The government's acknowledgment of its historical neglect of African Americans and, eventually, its enactment of a reparational sickling prevention program, which was allegedly desired by the black community, did not do away with the widespread perception among some blacks that any government intervention into black procreational practices must be a matter of population control. Clearly any program that assesses a risk has a eugenic dimension. It was the political problems posed by this dimension of screening that the government—while trying to mitigate its actions—ultimately was unable to solve. Those seeking the governance of sickling were more often than not met with cries of genocide and complaints about the heavy-handedness of government. During the hearings, mass screening and education were represented as needs coming out of the black community itself. It was argued that neighborhood organizations, churches, and various other local and national organizations had made sickling highly visible in the black community and that the government simply had to follow up on its expressed desires.

Nevertheless, the government's (sudden) interest in managing sickling was met with great suspicion by a great number of blacks. Mandatory mass genetic screening was seen by many as discriminating against blacks. Sickling was said to be commodified as information about the disease was being transformed into spectacle by the media (magazine headlines included "Incurable 'Negro Disease' Strikes Five in Family," "Sickle Cell Trait Rampant, But Ineffectual Among Black Footballers, Report Shows" and "Sickle Cell Hits Tar Heel Families"). To certain critics, the sickling program, which required a minimal outlay, was the ideal strategy for a government eager to appease discontented blacks who were fast becoming radicalized. Some have even suggested that the sickling program was part of President Nixon's election-year tactic to buy black votes. Far from representing the extension of full citizenship to African Americans—by defining the problems specific to that population as matters for which the collective social is responsible—the sickling program, according to these critics, was a family planning and population control program in disguise and had little to do with the preservation and welfare of blacks.[43]

These opposing discourses, while obviously complicating the

celebration of the proponents of the sickling program, also point to the existence of a community whose members perceived themselves to be marginalized, second-class citizens and who were suspicious of any government action on their behalf. In calling attention to these discourses, I am not suggesting that they are more—or less—adequate in addressing the political, ethical, medical, and semiotic demands of sickling. I simply want to indicate that the black community so carefully defined in the hearings through the testimonies of a cross-section of the black population was not in any essential way representative of a "real" unified community. In order to govern, as Nikolas Rose has pointed out, any liberal democratic government must "represent" a population by rendering it representable. In other words, a population—when governed—does not exist *except as* a governed entity. It is always ultimately an effect of its governance.[44]

*   *   *

In the 1970s, by depicting sickling as "a neglected disease afflicting citizens—African Americans—who were equally as neglected," the government provided itself with an occasion for demonstrating its will to represent the special interests of blacks, or to render blacks representable; however, in spite of the government's efforts to assure the support of the black community, not all blacks approved of the ways in which they were being represented. Eventually many blacks saw the governance of sickling as a conspiracy— as an insidious form of discrimination and even genocide. The isolation of the black population as the sole target of governance in the context of sickling was met with skepticism by many blacks. By singling out the black population for intervention, didn't the government contribute to—rather than discourage—the stigmatization of blacks? Given the fact that sickling did occur—albeit less frequently—in other populations, how could the government justify its exclusive focus on the black community? What were the possible implications—in terms of further discrimination—of this practice? In the 1970s several states considered introducing mandatory screening of their black citizens, many going so far as to require young children to undergo screening as a prerequisite for attending public school. Also, as screening programs were implemented around the country, carriers of the sickle cell trait were frequently denied jobs (as flight attendants, for instance, and in certain chemical industries), entrance into military academies (such as the Air Force), and insurance, because certain activities (such as flying or those entailing exposure to certain chemicals) were said to pose a considerable risk to those carrying the trait.

Mass screening for sickling, as it was practiced in the 1970s, took place at supermarkets, neighborhood clinics, churches (after services), and fairs and in other public spaces. The results were conveyed to the screened individuals in an ad hoc manner—most often through telephone calls or postcards. The information generated by the screenings was, in other words, circulating freely—and unconfidentially—in the public realm. One might say that the black body, once again, was put on public display. I am not suggesting that genetic information is of an essentially private nature. However, since the 1940s, a person's genetic makeup has been articulated as the watermark of his or her individuality, as the most private of properties, as the epitome of that which is assured government protection by the right to privacy. As such, it can be said to be the sine qua non of full citizenship. The fact that the screening results did not remain strictly confidential indicates that a private sphere—and therefore full citizenship—was not immediately available to blacks.

The information produced by the screenings was stored in genetic databases kept by the agencies that carried out the screenings, in local clinics and hospitals, and at various foundations for sickle cell anemia. Together, these dispersed databases inscribed African Americans as a population which was at once at risk and posing a potential risk to themselves and others when undertaking certain tasks required within specific work place settings.[45] They called into question the health of the carriers of the trait (which causes no symptoms) as the trait was being associated with risk.

This has led many critics to see the sickling project as an exemplary case of failed policy.[46] Such a position assumes that sickling exists, essentially, in a realm outside of discourse and is inherently manageable if the adequate techniques and tools are applied in the proper ways. In the view of these people, sickling, in the 1970s, became a public policy failure because the authorities did not do the preliminary work necessary to assure a smoothly running program. They failed to specify many details who could carry out screening and who could not; who was responsible for the dissemination of information about sickling; what kind of information should be conveyed; who should have access to the test results; who should provide individuals with genetic counseling; and what exactly the genetic counselors should tell carriers of the sickle cell trait.

My task here is not to try the government by assessing the degree of success or failure of the sickling initiative. In the context of a policy, failure is a purely discursive entity and cannot be quantified or objectively measured. To argue, as do some critics of the sickling program, that had the government addressed certain issues in advance, everything would have been all right and the policy would have been successful would be to suggest that sickling and the black citizen body can be separated from their social and political circumstances and the agendas of those involved and thus to grant them an independent "existence in nature"; and to imply that ideal policies can be implemented in "real" communities. Furthermore, it summons up an image of government as a seat of power from which society is administered and which can implement programs at will, yet in the case of the sickling initiative, governance was clearly a result of the activities of a diverse cadre of authorities, who urged ideas and actions upon politicians and legislators.

The dilemma facing the proponents of the sickling program was, as I have argued above, that no well-defined, unified black community existed at the time of the hearings and the enactment of the National Sickle Cell Anemia Prevention Act; rather, it had to be produced. The proponents of the sickling initiative sought to assemble a positive image of that which was to be governed—the black community—as well as to stress government's good intentions, organizing their presentation around such key terms as neglect (to be corrected), personal responsibility (presented as a universally available category to be appealed to), urgency (the insistence on immediacy being articulated as proof of the genuineness of government's concern for a group of marginalized citizens), and self-governance (as the crystallization of the benevolent nature of liberal democracy). The devices used to inscribe the black community ranged from illness narratives appearing in popular magazines to comparative socio-medical analyses of sickling and other diseases to testimonies by medical and public health experts and representatives of the alleged community.

However, devices of inscription, as both Rose and Latour have shown, do not have a neutral recording function; they are particular ways of acting upon a population.[47] By recording particular kinds of information (and organizing the recording around specific key terms), they produce a population amenable to particular forms of administration and intervention and render possible certain regimes for the conduct of conduct. In the case of sickling, a black community was inscribed which seemed to lend itself particularly well to the inexpensive, easily implementable, and very public procedure of mass screening. A prevention program targeting "the black community" was implemented with the declared aim of "protecting" and "preserving" the health of all Americans—and with the implied intention of confirming the status of African Americans as full members of the liberal democracy that is the United States. Ironically, the public response to the program was not one of universal approval.[48] The potential eugenic and discriminatory implications of screening seemed to confirm the status of blacks as lesser citizens, the argument went.

This chapter has interrogated the governance of a population through the "management" of a disease and examined the public response to such a project. It has shown that objectified and symbolically motivated, marginality or neglect is a positive, positioned product of power, and, once in place, as the effects of truth inscribed within interrelated discourses, make possible tactical interventions of surveillance and control.[49] It has also begun the task of problematizing the notion of "citizenship," which should be seen not merely as a function of rights, but as an effect of governance. The boundaries of citizenship are continuously redefined, as new modes of inscription create new spheres of reality and power.

Coda

The Italian novelist Italo Calvino tells the story about Mr. Palomar's visit to the Barcelona Zoo, the home of Snowflake, the only known exemplar of the great albino ape from equatorial Africa. Mr. Palomar is fascinated with the enormous gorilla whose gaze expresses "all the resignation at being the way he is, the sole exemplar in the world of a form not chosen."[1] Seated against a wall, Snowflake presses against his chest an old rubber tire:

What can this object be for him? A toy? A fetish? A talisman? Mr. Palomar feels he understands the gorilla perfectly, his need for something to hold tight while everything eludes him, a thing with which to allay the anguish of isolation, of difference, of the sentence of being always considered a living phenomenon.[2]

In the cage with Snowflake is a black female gorilla with a baby in her arms. She too has an old tire, but, as opposed to Snowflake, she sits in it, "sunbathing and delousing her infant." The female gorilla's relationship with her tire is "practical, . . . without problems," while Snowflake's contact with his is "somehow symbolic":

From it [the tire] he can have a glimpse of what for man is the search for an escape from the dismay of living—investing oneself in things, recognizing oneself in signs, transforming the world into a collection of symbols— a first daybreak of culture in the long biological night. . . . Looking at it [the tire], you would not say that much could be derived from it. And yet what, more than an empty circle, can contain all the symbols you might want to attribute to it?[3]

In Mr. Palomar's view, the quality of Snowflake's attachment to his tire is what most distinguishes him from the other gorillas in the cage. The fact that the tire to him has a meaning that lies beyond its practical function, signals his having access, however incomplete, to the realm of the symbolic—language. While the other gorillas exist in nature, Snowflake is emerging from the long biological night, he has reached the threshold of culture, he has begun the process of becoming human.

At the basis of Snowflake's particular relationship with the tire, which marks the transition from nature (Ape) to culture ([hu]-Man), is his experience of uniqueness—or difference.[4] Snowflake's need to identify with the old rubber tire is described as stemming from "the effort of bearing his own singularity, and the suffering at occupying space and time with his presence so cumbersome and evident." Since Snowflake is unique or different because of his "pink and glabrous skin, like that of a human of the white race," the story is, among other things, about the centrality to culture (or at least some (Western) cultures) of racial difference.[5]

The story about Mr. Palomar and Snowflake can be read as a parabolic expression of the conclusions about sickling and race that I have arrived at in this book. Throughout the twentieth century, sickling, like Snowflake and his old rubber tire, has existed in the indeterminate space between nature and culture, which in the West—as in the gorillas' "garden"—is also the locus of race and racial difference. While seeing themselves as describing a biological fact without symbolic potentiality, those researching sickling have consistently approached the phenomenon, like Snowflake approaches his tire, as an empty circle, able to contain all the symbols they wanted to attribute to it. More specifically, these researchers have used sickling to establish for the human body—in the authoritative languages of medicine, genetics, and physical anthropology, which presumably correspond *essentially* to what they describe—the distinction between nature (the nonwhite body that is still subject to natural selection) and culture (the white body on which natural selection has ceased to have any bearing). They have appropriated sickling to support the particular interpretation of the relationship between nature and culture without which the notion of race would cease to make sense.

Notes

Introduction

1. J. B. Herrick, "Peculiar Elongated and Sickle-Shaped Red Blood Corpuscles in a Case of Severe Anemia," *Archives of Internal Medicine*, 5 (1910), 517–521, p. 517.

2. V. E. Emmel, "A Study of the Erythrocytes in a Case of Severe Anemia with Elongated and Sickle-Shaped Red Blood Corpuscles," *Archives of Internal Medicine*, 20 (1917), 586–598.

3. V. R. Mason, "Sickle Cell Anemia," *Journal of the American Medical Association*, 79 (1922), 1318–1320.

4. See T. B. Cooley, "Likeness and Contrast in the Hemolytic Anemias of Childhood," *American Journal of Diseases of Children*, 33 (1928), 1257–1262.

5. R. Williams, *Textbook of Black-Related Diseases* (New York, 1975).

6. We do not know the incidence of sickle cell anemia in African Americans, but thanks to routine screenings of newborns we do know the incidence of carrying two copies of the sickle cell gene at birth. The best figures are 1 in 400 to 1 in 500, based on the heterozygote frequency in the United States of about 0.08 (8 percent). We can calculate the expected frequency of sickle cell anemia in African Americans at birth: $0.08 \times 0.08 \times 0.25 = .0016$. (Twenty-five percent is the odds that a couple, both of whom have sickle cell trait, will have a child with sickle cell anemia.)

7. K. Kipple and V. King, *Another Dimension to the Black Diaspora* (Cambridge, 1981).

8. We could theoretically eliminate many Mendelian phenomena from human populations (as they no longer confer any advantages, but exist because there is no reason for them not to do so) by influencing the reproductive behavior of the carriers of certain genes. This is the idea behind genetic testing and counseling of individuals who are "at risk" for hereditary diseases. Such a strategy is not merely a medico-technical problem but even more so a political matter.

9. I want to demonstrate that the discourse network within which a disease occurs is an integral part of the disease. I am not the first to make this type of argument. In a series of convincing papers published over two

decades ago, the British historian of medicine Karl Figlio argues that "disease as a clinical object structures a cluster of social relations, and [that] at the same time it is itself socially constructed" (K. Figlio, "Chlorosis and Chronic Disease in Nineteenth-Century Britain: The Social Constitution of Somatic Illness in a Capitalist Society," *International Journal of Health Services*, 8 [1978], 589–617). Writing in a different vein, the medical philosopher Marx W. Wartofsky states that "a disease, or a disease-syndrome, is the property or characteristic of a population, i.e., of a system of individuals in a given socio-historical context . . . it is *not* [to say] that the disease manifests itself . . . in anything other than individual persons; but rather that the very characterization of these individuals transcends their particularity. . . . The distinctiveness of the human individual . . . rests in his or her sociality and historicity. . . . The disease-syndrome . . . is therefore also to be defined as a socio-historical and cultural phenomenon; and the medical practice, whose domain is the treatment of disease, must be conceived accordingly" (M. Wartofsky, "Organs, Organisms and Disease: Human Ontology and Medical Practice," in H. T. Engelhardt, Jr., and S. F. Spicker [eds.], *Evaluation and Explanation in the Biomedical Sciences* [Dordrecht-Holland, 1975], 67–83).

10. S. Gilman, *The Case of Sigmund Freud: Medicine and Identity at the Fin de Siècle* (Baltimore, 1993).

11. The use of quotation marks around terms such as "Negro," "hybridity," and "race" has become mandatory among scholars informed by the notion that these terms designate discursively constructed rather than naturally occurring entities. These scholars, then, use quotation marks to challenge the essentializing representation implied by the unmarked usage of the terms. Although I agree with that strategy, I have elected, throughout this book, to use quotation marks sparingly. This is, on the one hand, for the sake of readability, on the other, because the book explicitly and exclusively analyzes the ways in which such terms as "Negro," "hybridity," and "race" are constituted in discourse and practice. Since my analysis details what the quotation marks merely suggest, I deem it appropriate to use only a few.

12. This book is based on the notion espoused by French critical thinkers such as Georges Canguilhem and Michel Foucault but most succinctly formulated by François Delaporte that disease does not exist outside of discourse and practice. François Delaporte, *Disease and Civilization: The Cholera in Paris, 1832* (Cambridge, 1986).

13. The dates listed in this passage are suggestive. Although the discourses I examine are most prominent in the literature at the specified points in time, they do not necessarily emerge for the first time at these times nor do they necessarily cease to exist past the specified periods.

14. See F. A. Kittler, *Discourse Networks, 1800/1900* (Stanford, 1990). See also F. Delaporte, *Disease and Civilization: The Cholera in Paris, 1832* (Cambridge, 1986), and K. Figlio, "How Does Illness Mediate Social Relations? Workmen's Compensation and Medico-Legal Practices, 1890–1940," in P. Wright and A. Treacher (eds.), *The Problem of Medical Knowledge* (Edinburgh, 1982), 174–223.

15. There is now a sizable body of literature on the subject of visualization and cognition, including: M. Douglas (ed.), *Essays in the Sociology of Perception* (London, 1982); M. Foucault, *The Birth of the Clinic: An Archaeology of Medical Perception*, trans. A. Sheridan (New York, 1973); J. Goody, *The Domestication of the Savage Mind* (Cambridge, 1977); B. Latour, "Visualization and Cognition: Thinking with Eyes and Hands," *Knowledge and Society*, 6 (1986), 1-40; M. Lynch, "Discipline and the Material Form of Images: An Analysis of Scientific Visibility," *Social Studies of Science*, 15, no. 1 (1985), 37-65; R. Rorty, *Philosophy and the Mirror of Nature* (Princeton, 1979); and M. Rudwick, "The Emergence of a Visual Language for Geological Science, 1760-1840," *History of Science*, 14 (1976), 149-195.

16. N. Rose, "Medicine, History and the Present," in C. Jones and R. Porter (eds.), *Reassessing Foucault: Power, Medicine, and the Body* (London, 1994), 48-72, p. 53.

17. P. Hirst, *On Law and Ideology* (Atlantic Highlands, N.J., 1979).

18. The literature here is considerable; for some useful examples of work of this kind, see the journal *Culture, Medicine and Psychiatry*. Recently there have been attempts to say more useful things in general about the "social" and not just about medicine, the body, pain, and the self—with varying degrees of success. On this score, see A. Kleinman, *The Illness Narratives: Suffering, Healing, and the Human Condition* (New York, 1986); *Rethinking Psychiatry: From Cultural Category to Personal Experience* (New York, 1988); A. Kleinman and J. Kleinman, "Suffering and its Professional Transformations: Toward an Ethnography of Experience," *Culture, Medicine and Psychiatry*, 15, no. 3 (1991), 275-301; M. J. Good, P. Brodwin, and A. Kleinman (eds.), *Pain as Human Experience: An Anthropological Perspective* (Berkeley, Los Angeles, London, 1992). See also the special issue of the journal—*Daedalus*, 125, no. 1 (1996).

19. T. Osborne, "On Anti-Medicine and Clinical Reason," in Colin Jones and Roy Porter (eds.), *Reassessing Foucault: Power, Medicine, and the Body*, pp. 28-47.

20. Michel Foucault, *The History of Sexuality*, vol. 1, *An Introduction*, trans. Robert Hurley (New York, 1980), 95-96.

21. Cultural anthropology has registered other forms of specification of social agents. E. Evans-Pritchard, in *Witchcraft, Oracles and Magic Among the Azande* [1937]/(Oxford, 1976), has shown that for the Azandes there is no single place from which the subject is hailed. This lack of a single locus of supervision suggests the moving of the prevailing social discourse away from the interior of the subject to her exteriority—to cultural obligations and techniques. For an interesting discussion of agency in these terms, see P. Hirst and P. Woolley, *Social Relations and Human Attributes* (London and New York, 1982), 136-137; N. Rose, *Inventing Our Selves: Psychology, Power, and Personhood* (Cambridge, 1996); G. Deleuze, *Foucault* (Minneapolis, 1988); and M. Taussig, *Mimesis and Alterity: A Particular History of the Senses* (New York and London, 1993), and "Reification and the Consciousness of the Patient," *Social Science and Medicine*, 14B (1986), 3-13. For a slightly different but related approach, see J. Butler, "For a Careful Reading," in S. Benhabib, J. Butler, D. Cornell, and N. Fraser (eds.), *Femi-*

nist Contentions: A Philosophical Exchange (New York, 1995), 127–143; and E. Grosz, *Volatile Bodies: Toward a Corporeal Feminism* (St. Leonards, 1994).

22. Kleinman, *Writing at the Margin*, 97.

23. Kleinman, *Writing at the Margin*, 98.

24. See P. Joyce, *Democratic Subjects: The Self and the Social in Nineteenth-Century England* (Cambridge, 1994), 12; J. W. Scott, "The Evidence of 'Experience,'" *Critical Inquiry*, 17 (Summer 1991), 773–797.

25. B. Good, *Medicine, Rationality, and Experience: An Anthropological Perspective* (Cambridge, 1994), is an articulate critique of the positivism underlying much of medical (anthropological) knowledge. But arguing, today, for a Saussurian distinction between sign and signified as established historically, does not advance the project far, as subjects are still seen as constructing meanings when in fact meaning could be said to construct subjects. So while a step has been taken out of the epistemological paradigms of clinical empiricism and positivism, Good retreats into another problematic paradigm—hermeneutics. But as Osborne so cogently shows, clinical positivism, far from being subversive of individuality (the "moral" individual), is precisely the science of individuality. Another problem, which I do not have space to address here, is that contemporary medicine is a site for the deployment of very diverse forms of expertise—including anthropological knowledge. It may be interesting to examine the various ways in which the "experts" construct illnesses/diseases as well as the terms they privilege in their respective analyses (objectivity, humanity, efficiency, moral worlds, and "experience-near," to mention but a few). See Rose, *Medicine, History, and the Present*, 50.

26. Hirst and Woolley, *Social Relations*, 138.

27. Prior to the 1970s there was no discourse on the "sickwo/man" in sickling. The sufferer was silent and not a part of the discussion about sickling.

28. For an excellent study along these lines, see James C. Faris, *Navajo and Photography: A Critical History of an American People* (Albuquerque, 1996).

Chapter 1. Interrogating Bodies

This title was borrowed from an editorial (similarly titled) appearing in a popular journal of the period. See editorial, "When Is a Caucasian Not a Caucasian?" *Independent* 70 (1911), 478–479.

Notes to epigraphs: R. Ellison, *Invisible Man* (New York, 1972 [1947]), 213. G. S. Graham, "A Case of Sickle Cell Anemia with Necropsy," *Archives of Internal Medicine*, 34, no. 6 (1924), 778–800.

1. The efficacy of the paradigms identified by McBride is not limited to the first half of the twentieth century, as we find elements of these paradigms in contemporary medical research.

2. D. McBride, *From TB to AIDS: Epidemics Among Urban Blacks Since 1900* (Albany, 1991), 32.

3. McBride, *From TB to AIDS*, 32.

4. McBride, *From TB to AIDS*, 32–33.

5. The term "discourse networks" as used here departs radically from McBride's paradigms—"sociomedical racialism" and "scientific epidemiology"—in that it does not represent a set program for research that comes from the outside and attaches itself to an object (in our case, sickling) that predates it. The object of study is not what is said or written but—as Foucault and Kittler would say—the fact "that this and not rather something else is inscribed." See M. Foucault, *Discipline and Punish: The Birth of the Prison* (London, 1977); F. Kittler, *Discourse Networks, 1800/1900* (Stanford, 1990).

6. V. R. Mason, "Sickle Cell Anemia," *Journal of the American Medical Association*, 79 (1922), 1318–1320, p. 1320.

7. See J. Huck, "Sickle Cell Anemia," *Bulletin of the Johns Hopkins Hospital*, 34 (1923), 335–344; V. P. Sydenstricker, W. A. Mulherin, and R. A. Houseal, "Sickle Cell Anemia," *American Journal of Diseases of Children*, 26 (1923), 132–154; V. P. Sydenstricker, "Further Observations on Sickle Cell Anemia," *Journal of the American Medical Association*, 83 (1924), 12–18.

8. G. Pollock, *Vision and Difference: Femininity, Feminism and Histories of Art* (New York, 1988).

9. T. B. Cooley, "Likenesses and Contrasts in the Hemolytic Anemias of Childhood," *American Journal of Diseases of Children*, 36 (1928), 1257–1262.

10. T. B. Cooley, "Likenesses and Contrasts," 1258.

11. V. Emmel, "A Study of the Erythrocytes in a Case of Severe Anemia with Elongated and Sickle-Shaped Red Blood Corpuscles," *Archives of Internal Medicine*, 20 (1917), 586–598.

12. The French philosopher Georges Canguilhem has provided one of the best analyses of how the laboratory came to replace the clinic as the privileged site for the production of medical knowledge. See his *On the Normal and Pathological*. See also A. Cunningham and P. Williams (eds.), *The Laboratory Revolution in Medicine* (Cambridge, 1992).

13. V. P. Sydenstricker et al., "Sickle Cell Anemia," 154.

14. V. P. Sydenstricker et al., "Sickle Cell Anemia," 154.

15. T. B. Cooley and P. Lee, "The Sickle Cell Phenomenon," *American Journal of Diseases of Children*, 32 (1926), 334–340, p. 334.

16. G. S. Graham and S. H. McCarty, "Notes on Sickle Cell Anemia," *Journal of Laboratory and Clinical Medicine*, 12 (1927), 536–547.

17. H. W. Josephs, "Sickle Cell Anemia," *Bulletin of the Johns Hopkins Hospital*, 40 (1927), 77–84.

18. K. Miyamoto and J. Korb, "Meniscocytosis (Latent Sickle-Cell Anemia): Its Incidence in St. Louis," *Southern Medical Journal*, 20 (1927), 912–916.

19. V. Castana, "Gigantociti e Le Anemie Semilunari," *La Pediatria*, 33 (1925), 431. Translation mine.

20. R. G. Archibald, "A Case of Sickle Cell Anemia in the Sudan," (translated) *Transactions of the Royal Society of Tropical Medicine and Hygiene*, 19 (1925–26), 389–393.

21. J. S. Lawrence, "Elliptical and Sickle-Shaped Erythrocytes in the Circulating Blood of White Persons," *Journal of Clinical Investigation*, 5 (1927), 31–49, p. 44.

22. W. B. Stewart, "Sickle Cell Anemia," *American Journal of Diseases of Children,* 34 (1927), 72–80, p. 75.

23. S. Rosenfeld and J. Pincus, "The Occurrence of Sicklemia in the White Race," *American Journal of Medical Sciences,* 184 (1932), 672–682, p. 676.

24. The image of Cuba (and by extension the Caribbean and Latin America) as a violent racial melting pot was used, in the United States, to counter Cubans' claim to whiteness. But it was also prevalent among the Cuban elite in Cuba eager to construct a racialized social order in the image of Euro-American society. In the nineteenth and early twentieth centuries, for example, the Cuban ruling class used modified European racial classifications to render governable the Cuban population. Complicating such old colonial racial notions as mulatto, mestizo, and zambo, they proclaimed the white Cuban prototype to be of "matte olive" coloration, presenting this fairly "dark" complexion as the mark of the tropical climate on an otherwise white body. See F. Ortiz, *Cuba y Su: Evolución Colonial* (Havana, 1967); V. Martinez-Alier, *Marriage, Class and Colour in Nineteenth-Century Cuba: A Study of Racial Attitudes and Sexual Values in a Slave Society* (London, 1974).

25. T. B. Cooley and P. Lee, "Sickle Cell Anemia in a Greek Family," *American Journal of Diseases of Children,* 38 (1929), 103–106, p. 105.

26. As Herzfeld has pointed out the status of the Greeks within European tradition is more often than not ambiguous in that it falls disconcertingly between the exotic ("nonwhiteness") and the familiar ("whiteness"). While there is no doubt as to the centrality of the Ancient Greeks in the European discourse on Europeanness (as opposed to Otherness), Modern Greeks do not fit comfortably into the duality of Europeans ("whites") and Others ("nonwhites"). As Herzfeld puts it: "For many West Europeans the Greeks of today are a people neither dramatically exotic nor yet unambiguously European."

27. G. S. Graham and S. H. McCarty, "Sickle Cell (Meniscocytic Anemia)," *Southern Medical Journal,* 23 (1930), 598–607, p. 600.

28. S. Rosenfeld and J. Pincus, "The Occurrence of Sicklemia," 674–681, p. 675.

29. Rosenfeld and Pincus, "The Occurrence of Sicklemia," p. 676.

30. Rosenfeld and Pincus, "The Occurrence of Sicklemia," p. 680.

31. P. R. Spickard, *Mixed Blood: Intermarriage and Ethnic Identity in Twentieth-Century America* (Madison, Wisc., 1989), 333. Also see J. D. Forbes, *Black Africans and Native Americans: Color, Race and Caste in the Evolution of Red-Black People* (Oxford and New York, 1988).

32. L. Greenwald, J. S. Spielholz, and J. Litmans, "Sickling Trait in a White Adult Associated with Hemolytic Anemia, Endocarditis and Malignancy," *American Journal of Medical Sciences,* 206 (1943), 158–168, pp. 158–159.

33. Greenwald, Spielholz, and Litmans, "Sickling Trait in a White Adult," 158–159.

34. M. A. Ogden, "Sickle Cell Anemia in the White Race," *Archives of Internal Medicine,* 71 (1943), 164–182, p. 178.

35. F. Clarke, "Sickle Cell Anemia in the White Race," *Nebraska Medical Journal*, 18 (1930), 376–379, p. 379.

36. J. Higham, *Strangers in the Land: Patterns of American Nativism, 1860–1925* (New York, 1963), especially chapter 10; Lothrop Stoddard, *The Rising Tide of Color Against White World Supremacy* (New York, 1922).

37. K. Roberts, "Why Europe Leaves Home" (Indianapolis, 1922), p. 22. Cited in J. Higham, *Strangers in the Land*, p. 273.

Chapter 2. The "Anthropathology" of the "American Negro"

1. I use the term "Negro" throughout this chapter (rather than the terms "black" or "African American") to refer not to a historical population or racial type, but rather to a discursive artifact specific to a certain time and place. The authors I quote (re-)invent, I would argue, the category of the "Negro," by defining the latter as an individual of compromised racial, ethnic, and biological integrity and using sickling as a "proof."

2. John S. Haller, *Outcasts from Evolution: Scientific Attitudes of Racial Inferiority, 1859–1900* (Urbana, 1971), 40–68. See also M. M. Torchia, "Tuberculosis among American Negroes: Medical Research on a Racial Disease, 1830–1950," *Journal of the History of Medicine* (July 1977), 252–279; D. McBride, *From TB to AIDS: Epidemics among Urban Blacks since 1900* (Albany, 1991).

3. A. Hrdlicka, "Anthropology and Medicine," *American Journal of Physical Anthropology*, 10 (1927), 206. For additional work on anthropology and medicine in relation to the "Negro," see Charles S. Johnson and Horace M. Bond, "The Investigation of Racial Differences Prior to 1910," *Journal of Negro Education*, 3 (1934), 328–339; W. Montague Cobbs, "The Physical Constitution of the American Negro," *Journal of Negro Education*, 3 (1934), 340–388; W. Montague Cobbs, "The Health Status and Health Education of Negroes in the United States," *Journal of Negro Education*, 6 (1937), 261–587.

4. S. J. Holmes, *The Negro's Struggle for Survival: A Study in Human Ecology* (Berkeley, 1937), 167–183.

5. See E. A. Hooton, "Progress in the Study of Race Mixtures with Special Reference to Work Carried On at Harvard University," *Proceedings of the American Philosophical Society*, 65 (1926), 312–323; A. Hrdlicka, "Anthropology of the American Negro: Historical Notes," *American Journal of Physical Anthropology*, 10 (1927), 205–235; A. Hrdlicka, "The Full-Blood American Negro," *American Journal of Physical Anthropology*, 12 (1928), 115–131; M. J. Herskovits, *The American Negro* (New York, 1930); M. F. A. Montagu, "Origins of the American Negro," *Psychiatry*, 7 (1944), 63–74; A. Meier, "A Study of the Racial Ancestry of the Mississippi College Negro," *American Journal of Physical Anthropology*, 7 (1949), 227–239; B. Glass and C. C. Li, "The Dynamics of Racial Intermixture: An Analysis Based on the American Negro," *American Journal of Human Genetics*, 5 (1953), 1–20; C. Stern, "Models Estimates of the Frequency of White and Near-White Segregants

in the American Negro," *Acta Genetica,* 4 (1953), 281–298; C. Stern, "The Biology of the Negro," *Scientific American,* 191 (1954), 81–85; D. F. Roberts, "The Dynamics of Racial Intermixture in the American Negro: Some Anthropological Considerations," *American Journal of Human Genetics,* 7 (1955), 361–367; and G. Myrdal, *An American Dilemma: The Negro Problem and Modern Democracy,* vol. 1 (New York, 1944), 113–136. All of these authors (while not presenting a unified position) organize their research around such concepts as interbreeding, intermixture, admixture, miscegenation, and hybridity.

6. See, for example, F. Tipton, "The Negro Problem from a Medical Standpoint," *New York Medical Journal,* 43 (1886), 569–572; Eugene R. Carson, "The Future of the Colored Race in the United States from an Ethnic and Medical Standpoint: Pt. 1," *New York Medical Times,* 15 (1887), 193–200; Frederick L. Hoffman, "Race Traits and Tendencies of the American Negro," *American Economic Association Publications,* 11 (1896), 1–329.

7. In many ways the notions of "the hybrid" and the "American Negro," as they were conceptualized in the early twentieth century, are comparable to the eighteenth- and nineteenth-century notion of the "degenerate" individual who, as the historian Elizabeth A. Williams so elegantly puts it, was seen as "inherit[ing] pathological proclivities worsened under the influence of a noxious environment . . . and . . . then pass[ing them] on to a yet more feeble progeny." E. A. Williams, *The Physical and the Moral: Anthropology, Physiology, and Philosophical Medicine in France, 1750–1850* (Cambridge, 1994), 15. See also R. A. Nye, *Crime, Madness, and Politics in Modern France: The Medical Concept of National Decline* (Princeton, 1994).

8. L. Hirszfeld and H. Hirszfeld, "Serological Differences Between the Blood of Different Races," *Lancet,* 197 (1919), 675–679.

9. J. H. Lewis and D. L. Henderson, "The Racial Distribution of Isohemagglutinin Groups," *Journal of the American Medical Association,* 79 (1922), 1422–1424; also, J. H. Lewis, *The Biology of the Negro* (Chicago, 1942), 82–98.

10. J. H. Lewis, "Race and Disease," *Proceedings of the Institute of Medicine of Chicago,* 17 (1948), 112–118.

11. Lewis, "Race and Disease," 113.

12. Lewis, "Race and Disease," 113.

13. W.E.B. DuBois, "The Health and Physique of the Negro American," *Atlanta University Publications,* 8–13 (1906), 4–112.

14. DuBois, "Health and Physique," 28–29.

15. Portraits were frequently used by African American scholars around the turn of the century as a means of staging the internal differentiation of the "Negro" population. See, for example, Booker T. Washington, N. B. Wood, and Fannie Barrier Williams, *A New Negro for A New Century* (New York, 1969 [1900]), which contains some sixty portraits.

16. DuBois pieces together statements by a wide range of anthropologists (such as F. Boas, J. Deniker, William Z. Ripley, and Giuseppe Sergi) and others who have problematized racial determinism. See "Health and Physique," 15.

17. DuBois, "Health and Physique," 89; DuBois is but one of the better

known African American and white American physicians engaging in a kind of sociomedical investigation whose primary goal was to examine the interaction of environment and health, and which thus represented a shift away from the notion of "racial disease" to that of "social disease." See R. Ruggles Gates, *Pedigrees of Negro Families* (Philadelphia, 1949); Holmes, *The Negro's Struggle for Survival*; A. G. Love and C. B. Davenport, "A Comparison of White and Colored Troops in Respect to Incidence of Disease," *Proceedings of the National Academy of Science*, 5 (1919), 58–67; Hoffman, "Race Traits and Tendencies of the American Negro."

18. My use of the terms "culturalist" and "racialist" is intended to situate my project alongside a growing body of work that approaches the question of race from the point of view of its discursive conditions. See, for example, Michael Omi and Howard Winant, *Racial Formation in the United States: From the 1960s to the 1980s* (New York, 1986); David Theo Goldberg (ed.), *Anatomy of Racism* (Minneapolis, 1990); Ronald T. Takaki, *Iron Cages: Race and Culture in Nineteenth-Century America* (New York, 1979); Reginald Horsman, *Race and Manifest Destiny: The Origins of American Racial Anglo-Saxonism* (Cambridge, 1981); David R. Roediger, *The Wages of Whiteness: Race and the Making of the American Working Class* (New York, 1991); Barbara J. Fields, "Ideology and Race in American History," in J. Morgan Kousser and James M. McPherson (eds.), *Region, Race and Reconstruction: Essays in Honor of C. Vann Woodward* (New York, 1982), 143–177; Thomas C. Holt, "Race, Race-making, and the Writing of History," *American Historical Review*, 100 (1995), 1–20; Ruth Frankenberg, *White Women, Race Matters: The Social Construction of Whiteness* (Minneapolis, 1993); and, Peggy Pascoe, "Miscegenation Law, Court Cases, and Ideologies of 'Race' in Twentieth-Century America," *Journal of American History* (June 1996), 44–69; Peter Wade, "'Race,' Nature and Culture," *Man* (n.s.) 28 (1993), 17–34.

19. I borrow this very useful phrase from the medical historian Paul Weindling, *Health, Race and German Politics Between National Unification and Nazism, 1870–1945* (Cambridge, 1989).

20. This was an "anthropathology" by aim rather than by name. While the work of certain colonial and American researchers can best be described as anthropathologies of the Negro, none said they were engaged in such a project. All, however, were familiar with the work of Lewis, as seen by their citations of his text, and claimed to be outlining the ethnological significance of sickling.

21. I borrow the term "medic" from the historian Megan Vaughan, *Curing their Ills: Colonial Power and African Illness* (Cambridge, 1991). It is appropriate to use here because most authors I discuss were serologists, zoologists, and physiologists, not physicians.

22. See J. V. Neel, "The Inheritance of Sickle Cell Anemia," *Science*, 110 (1949), 64–66. A later version appeared as "The Inheritance of the Sickling Phenomenon With Particular Reference to Sickle Cell Disease," *Blood*, 6 (1951), 389–412; and E. A. Beet, "The Genetics of the Sickle-Cell Trait in a Bantu Tribe," *Annals of Eugenics*, 14 (1949), 279–284.

23. A. B. Raper, "Sickle-Cell Disease in Africa and America: A Comparison," *Journal of Tropical Medicine and Hygiene*, 53 (1950), 49–53.

24. American physicians found sickle-shaped cells in the blood of African Americans at the rates of 6.6 and 10.8 percent for the pre-1932 and post-1932 years, respectively. The year 1932 is crucial because it marks the introduction of new screening agents and better organized and controlled screenings. See Lewis, *The Biology of the Negro*, 235; J. V. Neel, "The Population Genetics of Two Inherited Blood Dyscrasias in Man," *Cold Spring Harbor Symposia on Quantitative Biology*, 15 (1950), 148–151.

25. In Brazil, A. S. de Castro, "A Anemia de Hematias Falciformes," *Journal de Pediatria*, 1 (1934), 427, J. M. de Mendonca, "Meniscocitemia: Sua Frequencia No Brasil," *Brasil Medico*, 56 (1942), 382–384, and E. M. de Silva, "Estudos Sobre Indice de Siclemia," *Memorias do Instituto Oswaldo Cruz*, 42 (1945), 315–344, reported sickle-shaped cells in people of African descent at the rates of 12.8, 7.4, and 10.0 percent. In Colombia, B. Mera, "Preliminares del Estudio de la Meniscocitemia en Colombia," *Boletín de la Oficina Sanitaria Pan-Americana* 22 (1943), 680–682, reported a sickling rate of 9.4 percent. In Cuba, M. Chediak, J. C. Calderón, and G. P. Vargas, "Anemia á Hématis Falciformes: Contribución a su Estudio en Cuba," *Archivos de Medicina Interna Havana*, 5 (1939), 313–370, reported a rate of 5.7 percent. In Honduras, T. H. McGavack and W. M. German, "Sicklemia in the Black Carib Indian," *American Journal of Medical Science*, 208 (1944), 350–355, found a rate of 8.0 percent. In Curaçao, A. Van der Sar, "Sickle-Cell Disease," *Doc. Neerlandica et Indonesica Morbis Tropicis*, 1 (1949), 270–277 reported a rate of 11.7 percent.

26. In literature from the 1930s, 1940s, and 1950s—the term "ethnology" refers to a science concerned with the racial differentiation of peoples. Thus, "ethnic" group means "racial" group. For the authors whose work I analyze, ethnology and physical anthropology resonate with one another to such an extent that they cannot easily be separated. This, in turn, reflects the fact that the main concern of ethnology at this time was to identify the distinguishing physical attributes of the races.

27. R. W. Evans, "The Sickling Phenomenon in the Blood of West African Natives," *Transactions of the Royal Society of Tropical Medicine and Hygiene*, 37 (1944), 281.

28. Evans, "The Sickling Phenomenon," and "Anaemia Associated with Sickle Cell Trait in British West African Natives," *Transactions of the Royal Society of Tropical Medicine and Hygiene*, 39 (1945), 207–220; H. C. Trowell, "Sickle Cell Anaemia," *East African Medical Journal*, 22 (1945), 34–45; E. A. Beet, "Sickle Cell Disease in the Balovale District of Northern Rhodesia," *East African Medical Journal*, 23 (1946), 75–86, and "The Genetics of the Sickle-Cell Trait in a Bantu Tribe"; W. M. Robertson and G. M. Findlay, "Sickle-Cell Anaemia in West Africa," *Transactions of the Royal Society of Tropical Medicine and Hygiene*, 40 (1947), 435–446; A. B. Raper, "The Incidence of Sicklaemia," *East African Medical Journal*, 26 (1949), 281–282; H. Lehmann and A. H. Milne, "The Sickle Cell Trait in Relation to Hemoglobin Level and Anaemia," *East African Medical Journal*, 6 (1949), 247–254.

29. The Arab patient was described in R. G. Archibald, "A Case of Sickle Cell Anemia in the Sudan," *Transactions of the Royal Society of Tropical Medicine and Hygiene*, 19, no. 7 (1926), 389–393; the Indian in L. Berk and

G. M. Bull, "A Case of Sickle Cell Anemia in an Indian Woman," *Clinical Proceedings Journal*, 2 (1943), 147–152; and the others in A. Altmann, "Sickle Cell Anemia in a South African-Born European," *Clinical Proceedings Journal*, 4 (1945), 1–10.

30. Trowell, "Sickle Cell Anaemia," 34; Trowell is referring here to the clinical association between sickling and malaria rather than to the interaction between the two. The adaptation thesis—that carrying the sickle cell trait affords protection against malaria—had yet to be articulated.

31. Raper, "Incidence of Sicklaemia," 282.

32. Raper, "Sickle-Cell Disease in Africa and America," 49.

33. The titles of most early papers on sickling are indicative of the way many at the time understood the phenomenon, namely as peculiar elongated sickle-shaped red blood corpuscles with anemia.

34. The question of the normal and the pathological in the context of healthy (symptomless) individuals whose blood was found to contain sickle-shaped (abnormal) cells anticipates more current debates—spurred by modern clinical genetics—about how to draw the line between health and disease. What does it mean to have no symptoms while possessing genes for certain diseases? Definitions of the normal and the pathological are, of course, always more than a mere medico-technical matter. During the 1970s, for example, when the sickle cell trait was pathologized many insurance companies, employers, and some branches of the U.S. armed services refused African Americans who had the trait on the grounds that they had "medical problems." This led to charges of discrimination, and eventually the trait was de-pathologized, a process that was as political as it was medical. That is, it was dropped as a medical risk.

35. V. P. Sydenstricker, "Sickle-Cell Anemia," *Southern Medical Journal*, 17 (1924), 177–183.

36. T. B. Cooley and P. Lee, "The Sickle Cell Phenomenon," *American Journal of Diseases of Children*, 32, no. 3 (1926), 334–340.

37. Constitutional medicine views disease as a function of specific inherited physical characters. An individual will get the diseases to which he or she is constitutionally predisposed. The environment is understood to play a negligible role in disease development.

38. G. S. Graham and S. H. McCarty, "Sickle Cell (Meniscocytic) Anemia," *Southern Medical Journal*, 23, no. 7 (1930), 600.

39. J. Bauer and L. J. Fisher, "Sickle Cell Disease—with Special Regards to Its Nonanemia Variety," *Archives of Surgery*, 47 (1943), 553–563.

40. Bauer and Fisher and Graham and McCarty use the term "status degenerativus" to refer to more than the peculiar symptoms of sickle cell anemia: they mean an inherited constitution that predisposes an individual (or family) to specific conditions. Writing in the second edition of his widely accepted text on constitutional medicine, *Constitution and Disease: Applied Constitutional Pathology* (New York, 1945), Bauer puts the matter this way: "It can hardly be considered as mere coincidence that patients affected with sickle cell disease were reported to have in addition various constitutional abnormalities other than sickle cell trait, such as thyreoglossal cysts, congenital cysts and abnormal fissures of the lungs;

just how often the sickle cell trait is only part of status degenerativus is not known" (153).

41. G. S. Graham, "A Case of Sickle Cell Anemia with Necropsy," *Archives of Internal Medicine*, 34, no. 6 (1924), 778–800.

42. Daniel J. Kevles, *In the Name of Eugenics* (New York, 1985), 176.

43. In 1949, Pauling and his colleagues (H. A. Itano, S. J. Singer, and I. C. Wells), studying the migration of hemoglobin in electric fields, observed that sickle-shaped red blood cells contained an altered form of hemoglobin that migrates less rapidly than normal hemoglobin (Hb A). Based on this observation, they traced the alteration in the shape of the red blood cells (from concave to sickle) to the modification of a hemoglobin that they named Hb S. Their study also confirmed Beet and Neel's hypothesis that sickling was a genetic phenomenon that when inherited from one parent produced the benign sickle cell trait, but when inherited from both parents resulted in sickle cell anemia. See L. Pauling, H. A. Itano, S. J. Singer, and I. C. Wells, "Sickle Cell Anemia: A Molecular Disease," *Science*, 110 (1949), 543–548.

44. See A. Montagu, *Man's Most Dangerous Myth* (Cleveland, 1964).

45. Garland E. Allen, "Old Wine in New Bottles: From Eugenics to Population Control in the Work of Raymond Pearl," in Keith R. Benson, Jane Maienschein, and Ronald Rainger (eds.), *The Expansion of American Biology* (New Brunswick, N.J., 1991), 231–261; Nancy L. Stepan, *The Hour of Eugenics* (Ithaca, N.Y., 1991).

46. Diane B. Paul, *Controlling Human Heredity: 1865 to the Present* (Atlantic Highlands, 1995), 124.

47. In 1950 at a gathering of physical anthropologists and human geneticists at Cold Spring Harbor, New York, Sherwood L. Washburn (dubbed the father of modern biological anthropology) proclaimed the birth of the "New Physical Anthropology" (see *Cold Spring Harbor Symposia on Quantitative Biology*, 15 [1950]). The new discipline was to incorporate the theories as well as the tools of molecular biology and genetics for comparative purposes, be it between humans and animals or between human populations. Also in 1950, the anthropologist William C. Boyd published his influential book, *The Genetics of Races* (Boston, 1950), in which he chided his fellow physical anthropologists for, among other things, not incorporating gene frequencies (that is blood groups) into their study of race.

48. Raper, "Sickle Cell Disease in Africa and America," 50.

49. Raper, "Sickle Cell Disease in Africa and America," 52.

50. Raper, "Sickle Cell Disease in Africa and America," 53.

51. Raper, "Sickle Cell Disease in Africa and America," 53.

52. The geneticist-eugenicist R. Ruggles Gates cited Raper and Lehmann to contest the UNESCO proclamation of September 7, 1951, that "there is no evidence that race mixture produces disadvantageous results from a biological point of view." See his article "Disadvantages of Race Mixture," *Nature*, 170 (November 22, 1952), 896.

53. Biomedicine had confirmed sickling's status as a disease of the "Negro blood," but had had to construct the category of the "apparently

white individual" to do so. How else could one account for the fact that sickling did indeed occur in phenotypically "white" individuals? It is interesting that biomedicine should afford such a central role to the category of the "apparently white individual" insofar as the latter is not a medical category but an ethnological one. The fact that biomedicine so readily appropriated a term from the field of ethnology effectively undermines its claim to objectivity. Biomedicine, no less than any other science, has a stake in the discourse networks that constitute the prevailing Zeitgeist.

54. McGavack and German, "Sicklemia in the Black Carib Indian," 350.

55. McGavack and German, "Sicklemia in the Black Carib Indian," 351. Taylor was an anthropologist working among the Caribs. See D. Taylor, "Columbus Saw Them First," *Natural History*, 48 (1941), 40–49.

56. McGavack and German, "Sicklemia in the Black Carib Indian," 350.

57. McGavack and German, "Sicklemia in the Black Carib Indian," 351.

58. German and McGavack attribute the "racial integrity" and bodily health of the Black Caribs to their "customs and moral standards," thus suggesting a link between moral and racial hygiene, on the one hand, and the health of the individual (as well as the overall social) body, on the other.

59. The study of the Black Caribs (the Garifuna) from an anthropathological perspective continues. See M. Crawford (ed.), *Current Developments in Anthropological Genetics, Vol. 3: Black Caribs* (New York, 1984).

60. Raper, "Sickle Cell Disease in Africa and America," 51–52.

61. Neel, "The Population Genetics of Two Inherited Blood Dyscrasias in Man," 149–151.

62. In a memoir examining sixty-two years of his work in human genetics—*Physician to the Gene Pool: Genetic Lessons and Other Stories* (New York, 1994)—Neel revisits the debate: "A. B. Raper and H. Lehmann suggested that the admixture between Negro and Caucasian that had occurred in the U.S. was somehow responsible for the high prevalence of the overt anemia. The issue was resolved in two ways. In 1951 and 1952 . . . the Labotte-Legrands [working in the Congo] showed that when one concentrated attention on young children, the frequency of the anemia really was as high as predicted. In the meantime, in the U.S., I could demonstrate no relationship between the apparent degree of white admixture in African-Americans and the manifestations of the sickling gene, thus casting doubt on the alternative explanation suggested above" (47).

63. The concept of race has survived a number of paradigmatic shifts within the sciences. Even scientific discourses within which race has no explanatory value have often co-existed with—and sometimes contributed to—the perpetuation of the concept. Darwinian biology is a case in point. This reflects the interdependence of scientific and other discourses, and points to the absurdity of the notion of pure science.

64. In using the nineteenth-century meaning of "North America" in 1948, Switzer and Fouche keep alive a discourse according to which any difference between African Americans in the South and those in the North with respect to a host of attributes including disease and hygienic practices can be explained by supposed radical biological difference, the

northern group being the less "degenerate" of the two. See John S. Haller's excellent *Outcasts from Evolution,* especially chapter II: "The Physician versus the Negro," 40–68.

65. P. K. Switzer and H. H. Fouche, "Sickle Cell Trait: Incidence and Influence in Pregnant Colored Women," *American Journal of Medical Science,* 216 (1948), 332.

66. The journal *Blood* was founded in the late 1940s by the American Society of Hematology. It reflects the emerging significance of the experimental methodology in medicine and the growing importance of the red blood cell and hemoglobin as research tools.

67. J. H. Hodges, "The Effect of Racial Mixtures upon Erythrocytic Sickling," *Blood,* 5, no. 9 (1950), 804.

68. Hodges, "Effect of Racial Mixtures," 804.

69. L. W. Diggs, C. F. Ahmann, and J. Bibb, "The Incidence and Significance of the Sickle Cell Trait," *Annals of Internal Medicine,* 7 (1933), 774.

70. Diggs, Ahmann, and Bibb, "Incidence and Significance of the Sickle Cell Trait," 772.

71. For critical discussions of the literature see Mary V. Dearborn's *Pocahontas' Daughters: Gender and Ethnicity in American Culture* (New York, 1986); Lora Romero, "Vanishing Americans: Gender, Empire, and New Historicism," in S. Samuels (ed.), *The Culture of Sentiment: Race, Gender, and Sentimentality in Nineteenth-Century America* (New York, 1992); Karen Sanchez-Eppler, "Bodily Bonds: The Intersecting Rhetoric of Feminism and abolition," *Representation,* 24 (1988), 28–59; for an analysis focusing on the most recent past, see the work of the anthropologist Virginia Dominguez, *White by Definition: Social Classification in Creole Louisiana* (New Brunswick, N.J., 1986).

72. Hodges, "Effect of Racial Mixtures," 804–805.

73. Hodges, "Effect of Racial Mixtures," 805.

74. Hodges, "Effect of Racial Mixtures," 809.

75. Hodges, "Effect of Racial Mixtures," 809.

76. R. Ashman, "Are Certain Blood Dyscrasias an Effect of Racial Mixtures?" *American Journal of Physical Anthropology* (n.s.), 10 (1952), 217, 218.

77. Ashman, "Certain Blood Dyscrasias," 219. Ashman dismisses the notion of a selective advantage for the heterozygote on the grounds that the weight of available evidence points more in the direction of a selective disadvantage; he discounts mutation on the grounds that the high rate necessary to maintain the gene, although theoretically possible, is improbable; and he rejects the possibility of genetic drift because, with the exception of albinism among the San Blas Indians of Panama, no other account of this phenomenon is known.

78. Ashman, "Certain Blood Dyscrasias," 219.

79. J. A. Mjoen, the Norwegian eugenicist, is a prime representative of this discourse: "[I]t is not my opinion that hybridization will set a lower limit for the racial and cultural amalgamation of two different races in a community only because the hybrids become less fertile, but also because their physical and psychic health, their adaptability and their immunity are reduced as a result of frequent disharmonies in the combination

of hereditary qualities. . . . My observations among mixed populations, conclude that there is a causal relation between race-mixture and diminished immunity," in "Biological Consequences of Race-Crossing," *Journal of Heredity*, 17, no. 5 (1926), 175–185.

80. Ashman, "Certain Blood Dyscrasias," 219.
81. Ashman, "Certain Blood Dyscrasias," 200.
82. Ashman, "Certain Blood Dyscrasias," 220.
83. Ashman, "Certain Blood Dyscrasias," 220.
84. Ashman, "Certain Blood Dyscrasias," 222.

Chapter 3. Medical Problems with Ethnological Solutions

1. Michel Foucault, *The History of Sexuality*, vol. 1, *An Introduction*, trans. Robert Hurley (New York, 1980), 25.
2. Foucault, *The History of Sexuality*, 147.
3. Foucault, *The History of Sexuality*, 147.
4. Foucault, *The History of Sexuality*, 149.
5. The shift from language to blood as a basis for the categorization of peoples does not necessarily correspond to a shift from culture to biology. In the view of nineteenth-century linguists, working prior to the Saussurian revolution that divorced the science of language from everyday speech, languages occurred independently of culture and were governed by natural laws. Languages were seen as having specific territorial forms, such as nations or tribes. Consider the equation: one nation/people, one language. The spirit, the will, or racial essences in blood were seen as undergirding this naturalist nationalism. By the late nineteenth century, European ethnologists in Africa, unable to come to terms with the bilingual nature of certain peoples, sought to explain this state of affairs in terms of conquest and admixture of blood. See P. Lamoise, *Grammaire de la Langue Serere* (Saint-Joseph de Ngasobil, 1873); cited in S. Gal, "The Boundaries of Languages and Disciplines: How Ideologies Construct Difference," *Social Research* 62 (1995), 967–1002, p. 971. Recent work by anthropological and population geneticists establishing the worldwide migration of populations shows that we have yet to fully emerge from the naturalist view of language and its linkage with blood. See L. L. Cavalli-Sforza, *The Great Human Disaporas: A History of Diversity* (Reading, Mass., 1995); and R. Sokal et al., "Genetic Differences Among Language Families in Europe," *American Journal of Physical Anthropology* 79 (1989), 489–501.
6. For studies that bear directly on my work, see John and Jean Comaroff, *Ethnography and the Historical Imagination* (Boulder, Colo., 1992), especially chapter 8: "Medicine, Colonialism, and the Black Body," 215–233; S. Gilman, *Pathology and Difference: Stereotypes of Sexuality, Race and Difference* (Ithaca, 1985); R. Packard, "The 'Healthy Reserve' and the 'Dressed Native': Discourses on Black Health and the Language of Legitimation in South Africa," *American Ethnologist*, 16 (1989), 77–93; M. Vaughan, *Curing Their Ills: Colonial Power and African Illness* (Palo Alto, 1991). But also V. Y. Mudimbe, *The Invention of Africa: Gnosis, Philosophy, and the Order of Knowl-*

edge, (Bloomington, 1988); C. Miller, *Blank Darkness: Africanist Discourse in French* (Chicago, 1985).

7. Vaughan, *Curing Their Ills*, 81.

8. Vaughan, *Curing Their Ills*, 81.

9. R. Packard and P. Epstein, "Epidemiologists, Social Scientists, and the Structure of Medical Research on AIDS in Africa," *Social Science & Medicine* 33 (1991), 771–795.

10. T. B. Cooley and Pearl Lee, "The Sickle Cell Phenomenon," *American Journal of Diseases of Children*, 32 (1926), 340.

11. Johannes Fabian offers an excellent discussion of this discursive project, showing how anthropology constructs its Others by placing them in a different time. But his thesis is equally applicable, it seems, to medico-genetic discourse on Africa. See J. Fabian, *Time and the Other: How Anthropology Makes Its Object* (New York, 1983).

12. As cultural anthropology before it, physical anthropology has embarked on its own salvaging program—the Human Genome Diversity Project. This elaborate enterprise was originally given life by Cavalli-Sforza and the late Allen Wilson and is now carried forward with zest by Kenneth Weiss (Penn State), Mary-Claire King (University of California, Berkeley), Kenneth Kidd (Yale), and Marcus Feldman (Stanford). It is intended to collect twenty-five blood samples from some four hundred "tribal" peoples from various parts of the world who the proponents of the enterprise claim to be genetically "endangered." That is, human populations who are considered to be in danger of extinction or having their genetic "purity" (recalling another, racial "purity") lost due to mixing with their neighbors. See K. Weiss, "Biological Diversity Is Inherent in Humanity," *Cultural Survival Quarterly*, 20 (Summer 1996), 26–28; L. Roberts, "Anthropologists Climb (Gingerly) on Board," *Science*, 258, (1992), 1300–1301.

13. See, for example: J. Willis, "The Administration of Bonde, 1920–60: A Study of the Implementation of Indirect Rule in Tanganyika," *African Affairs*, 92 (1993), 53–68; A. Mafeje, "The Ideology of Tribalism," *Journal of Modern African Studies*, 9 (1971), 253–261; M. Mamdani, "Indirect Rule, Civil Society, and Ethnicity: The Africa Dilemma," *Social Justice*, 23 (1996), 145–151. In 1925, upon assuming the governorship of Tanganyika (present-day Tanzania), Sir Donald Cameron, who was among the first colonial administrators to implement that particular form of governance in East Africa, defined it as the practice of "administer[ing] the people through the instrument of their own indigenous institutions," that is, their own tribal institutions. (As cited by J. Graham, "Indirect Rule: The Establishment of 'Chiefs' and 'Tribes' in Cameron's Tanganyika," *Tanzania Notes and Records*, 77–78 [1976], 1–9, p. 3). But indirect rule was not easily implemented. If tribal units were to be the primary means for governing Africa, tribes had to be rendered knowable, countable, manipulable. The problem was, as the historian James D. Graham points out, that the inhabitants of any given African territory did not necessarily constitute "tribes" so much as infiltrations and migrations of sections of ethnic groups (see his "Indirect Rule," 5). What colonial administrators delineated as "tribes" did not necessarily correspond to any pre-existing social

organization. Africans may eventually have come to see themselves as belonging to the distinct "tribes" defined by the colonial administration. However, this sense of belonging should be seen as the effect rather than the cause of tribalism.

14. J. Iliffe, *A Modern History of Tanganyika* (Cambridge, 1979), 38.

15. L. Hirszfeld and H. Hirszfeld, "Serological Differences between the Blood of Different Races: The Results of Researches on the Macedonian Front," *Lancet*, 2 (1919), 675–679.

16. R. G. Archibald, "A Case of Sickle Cell Anemia in the Sudan," *Transactions of the Royal Society of Tropical Medicine and Hygiene*, 19 (1925–26), 389–393.

17. Editorial, "Sickle Cell Anaemia," *East African Medical Journal*, 22 (1945), 33.

18. R. Winston Evans, "The Sickling Phenomenon in the Blood of West African Natives," *Transactions of the Royal Society of Tropical Medicine and Hygiene*, 37 (1944), 281–286; and G. M. Findlay, W. Muir Robertson, and F. J. Zacharias, "The Incidence of Sicklaemia in West Africa," *Transactions of the Royal Society of Tropical Medicine and Hygiene*, 40 (1946), 83–86.

19. In 1952, the *British Medical Journal* (2 [1952], 433–434) ran another editorial on sickle cell anemia in Africa in which it attempted to show that the two opposing views were not mutually exclusive. Given Lehmann and Cutbush's thesis that the sickling gene was recently introduced to Africa from India, the editor claimed that not enough time had passed for the rates of the anemia to have reached the frequency one would have expected based on the genetic thesis.

20. Editorial, "Sickle Cell Anaemia," *East African Medical Journal*, 22 (1945), 33.

21. See D. Haraway, *Primate Visions: Gender, Race, and Nation in the World of Modern Science* (London, 1989), for the role of science in this regard. A number of medical historians have pointed out how early tropical medicine was characterized by a concern with vectors and pathogens rather than people and politics. Just when this division of early and presumably "late" tropical medicine came about is not clear. However, my argument is that in the 1940s colonial medicine was very much concerned with populations, politics, and history. See Vaughan, *Curing Their Ills*; S. M. Mackenzie, "Experts and Amateurs: Tsetse, Nagana, and Sleeping Sickness in East and Central Africa," in J. MacKenzie (ed.), *Imperialism and the Natural World* (Manchester, 1990), 187–212; L. White, "Tsetse Visions: Narratives of Blood and Bugs in Colonial Northern Rhodesia, 1931–9," *Journal of African History*, 36 (1995), 219–245.

22. H. C. Trowell, "Sickle Cell Anemia," *East African Medical Journal*, 22 (1945), 34–45, p. 34.

23. I do not view Trowell's freely travelling slave as an empirically grounded fact to be refuted, but as a notion that was necessary at this point in time for the maintenance of colonial medical discourse.

24. C. G. Seligman, *Races of Africa* (London, 1939), 55.

25. H. C. Trowell, "Sickle Cell Anaemia," 34.

26. H. C. Trowell, "Sickle Cell Anaemia," 34.

27. R. Winston Evans, "The Sickling Phenomenon in the Blood of West African Natives"; and G. M. Findlay, W. Muir Robertson, and F. J. Zacharias, "The Incidence of Sicklaemia in West Africa."

28. These terms were used by colonial administrators in Northern Rhodesia to describe the Lunda and Lovale people who were also the object of Beet's investigations. See R. Papstein, "From Ethnic Identity to Tribalism: The Upper Zambesi Region of Zambia, 1830–1931," in L. Vail (ed.), *The Creation of Tribalism in Southern Africa* (Berkeley, 1989), 378.

29. In "Healing and Curing: Issues in the Social History and Anthropology of Medicine in Africa," *Social History of Medicine*, 7 (1994), 283–295, M. Vaughan, a medical historian working in Uganda, argues that colonial medicine favored the "tribe" over the individual as its primary unit of analysis. More specifically, she shows how "culture and race took over, not simply as mediators of disease, but sometimes as sources of disease in themselves" (p. 289). See also her *Curing Their Ills*, where she argues that colonial medical discourse associated leprosy with the "breakdown of tribal authority" (82).

30. In "The Illusion of Tribe" (*The Passing of Tribal Man in Africa* [Leiden, 1970], 28–50), Aidan W. Southall puts it this way: "[H]ow ever much it wounds our romantic souls . . . the term 'tribe' should usually be applied only to the small-scale societies of the past which retained their political autonomy, and . . . the new associations derived from them in the contemporary context should be referred to as ethnic groups" (48).

31. E. A. Beet, "Sickle Cell Disease in the Balovale District," *East African Medical Journal*, 23 (1946), 75–86, p. 76.

32. Beet, "Sickle Cell Disease in the Balovale District," 75.

33. Beet, "Sickle Cell Disease in the Balovale District," 75.

34. Vaughan, *Curing Their Ills*, 81.

35. Because of the high incidence of anemia among Africans, the hematocrit values established as "normal" for the European body were deemed invalid for the African body. The hematocrit value measures the volume of packed red blood cells occurring when blood is centrifuged to cause the cells to settle.

36. Beet compares his findings with those of R. Winston Evans (1944) who had examined the blood of 561 West African ("Askari") soldiers coming from the "races" (as he called them) of Nigeria, the Cameroons, the Gold Coast, and Gambia and found a sickling rate of 19.9 percent, and those of G. M. Findlay (n.d.) who found the "incidence" among 300 Gold Coast "Askari" to be 15.5 percent.

37. Beet, "Sickle Cell Disease in the Balovale District," 79.

38. Beet, "Sickle Cell Disease in the Balovale District," 82.

39. Beet, "Sickle Cell Disease in the Balovale District," 82.

40. This (medical) way of looking at the Other and Elsewhere has not changed considerably since then. The latest research on sickling examined here is from 1992; its outlook does not differ significantly from that of the colonial medical enterprise. (I am of course aware that the notion that "tribes" are central components of the social predates its application to sickling.)

41. Beet, "Sickle Cell Disease in the Balovale District," 82.

42. Beet, "Sickle Cell Disease in the Balovale District," 83.

43. Beet, "Sickle Cell Disease in the Balovale District," 83.

44. Beet, "Sickle Cell Disease in the Balovale District," 84.

45. I shall leave unexamined the notion that the Luvale are fishers who favor the woodlands of the Kalahari, while the Lunda are hunters who also farm in the dense fertile grounds of the Chavuma area. One could obviously argue that the Luvale are significantly more likely to be exposed to the malaria parasite, *P. falciparum*. While Beet does suggest such a line of reasoning (he had earlier calculated the incidence of sickling in relation to malaria), pursuing this argument here would risk replacing one criterion for classification ("tribe") with another ("malaria").

46. Papstein, "From Ethnic Identity to Tribalism," 378.

47. Papstein, "From Ethnic Identity to Tribalism," 378.

48. Papstein, "From Ethnic Identity to Tribalism," 378.

49. Papstein, "From Ethnic Identity to Tribalism," 378.

50. Papstein, "From Ethnic Identity to Tribalism," 378.

51. E. A. Beet, "Sickle Cell Disease in the Balovale District," 85.

52. C. M. N. White quoted in E. A. Beet, "Sickle Cell Disease in the Balovale District," 85. C. M. N. White was the author of two publications on the Balovale District: "The Balovale Peoples and Their Historical Background," *Rhodes-Livingstone Journal*, 8 (1949), 26–41, and "Notes on the Political Organization of the Kabompo District and Its Inhabitants," *African Studies*, 9 (1950), 185–193.

53. See T. Asad (ed.), *Anthropology and the Colonial Encounter* (London, 1985); and for an attempt at a very fascinating but unnecessarily underdeveloped project, see D. Scott, "Colonial Governmentality," *Social Text*, 43 (1995), 191–220.

54. G. Brown and A. Bruce Hutt, *Anthropology in Action: An Experiment in the Iringa District of the Iringa Province Tanganyika Territory* (London, 1935).

55. Sir Philip Mitchell, foreword, in Brown and Bruce Hutt, *Anthropology in Action*, xi.

56. Sir Philip Mitchell, foreword, in Brown and Bruce Hutt, *Anthropology in Action*, xiii.

57. Sir Philip Mitchell, foreword, in Brown and Bruce Hutt, *Anthropology in Action*, xv.

58. E. A. Beet, "The Genetics of the Sickle-Cell Trait in a Bantu Tribe," *Annals of Eugenics*, 14 (1949), 279–284.

59. D. Armstrong, *Political Anatomy of the Body: Medical Knowledge in Britain in the Twentieth Century* (Cambridge, 1983), 11.

60. The historic significance of comparative ethnology in relation to medicine—including pathological anatomy, medical geography, and epidemiology—can be seen in the case of sleeping sickness (caused by the parasite *Trypanosoma Gambiense*). As early as the first decade of the twentieth century, medical geographers and epidemiologists working on the epidemic of that disease, attributed its rapid spread to the fact that the local populations were becoming increasingly migratory as a result of forced relocation of labor and colonial pacification strategies. In a manner typi-

cal of his time, F. M. Sandwith, a medical officer in Africa, summarized what "we knew about sleeping sickness," tendering that prior to the colonial system the social and geographical conditions of African living were such that they afforded a sort of cultural and natural *cordon sanitaire* for disease because "each tribe was at war with its neighbour, and no man ventured more than a few miles from his native villages; these villages, should they be infected, would in themselves become segregation camps." Sandwith was of the opinion that once this way of life had been destroyed, the parasite for sleeping sickness was carried by people from "tribe to tribe." See F. M. Sandwith, "What We Know About Sleeping Sickness," *Medical Press*, 146 (1912), 402–406, p. 405. Cited in M. Worboys, "The Comparative History of Sleeping Sickness in East and Central Africa, 1900–1914," *History of Science*, 32 (1994), 89–102, p. 91. Interestingly, Sandwith sees social change—rather than mosquitoes—as the most significant cause of sleeping sickness. Disease, he seems to be saying, is conditioned by the social rather than the physical environment. For an excellent analysis of this way of seeing and its application to tuberculosis and the body of the African miner, see A. Butchart, "The Industrial Panopticon: Mining in the Medical Construction of the Migrant African Labour in South Africa, 1900–1950," *Social Science and Medicine*, 42 (1996), 185–197; see also P. D. Curtin, "Medical Knowledge and Urban Planning in Colonial Tropical Africa," *American Historical Review*, 90 (1985), 594–613.

61. In 1945, H. C. Trowell had proclaimed that "no blood-count on an African can be considered complete unless a sealed drop preparation is made and examined for sickle cells" (Trowell, "Sickle Cell Anaemia," 42). E. A. Beet echoed this view when stating, a year later, that "no routine laboratory examination on an African is complete unless the simple test for sickling in vitro is carried out" (Beet, "Sickle Cell Disease in the Balovale District," 80). Three years after Beet, Alan B. Raper, a physician working in Uganda, warned that "it deserves emphasis that in Africa a test for sickling forms part of the basic examination of African patients without which his reaction to adverse conditions cannot be gauged" (A. B. Raper, "Sudden Death in Sickle Cell Disease," *East African Medical Journal*, 26 [1949], 14–22).

62. Beet, "The Genetics of the Sickle-Cell Trait in a Bantu Tribe," 280.

63. Beet, "The Genetics of the Sickle-Cell Trait in a Bantu Tribe," 280.

64. Beet, "The Genetics of the Sickle-Cell Trait in a Bantu Tribe," 280.

65. Lehmann, who received an M.D. as well as a Ph.D., was a chemical pathologist with the Royal Army Medical Corps between 1943 and 1947. In 1946, he was sent by the Corps to work in the laboratory of E. G. Holmes at Makerere College, where physiological research with special attention to malnutrition, anemias, and changes of the liver was being conducted. Although his stay in Holmes's laboratory lasted only a year, Lehmann remained at Makerere College until 1951, when he left to assume a position at St. Bartholomew's Hospital in London. During his career, which lasted well into the 1980s, Lehmann received numerous awards, including the 1963 Rivers Medal for Anthropological Work given by the Royal

Anthropological Institute. Lehmann's career strikes me as one that was given a boost by the colonial medical system. The experience he gained in Africa positioned him not only for the job at St. Bartholomew's but also for subsequent work on the abnormal hemoglobins at Cambridge, where he headed the Medical Research Council Abnormal Haemoglobin Unit.

66. H. Lehmann, "The Sickle-Cell Trait: Not an Essentially Negroid Feature," *Man*, 51–53 (1951–53), 9–10.

67. H. Lehmann and A. B. Raper, "Distribution of the Sickle-Cell Trait in Uganda, and Its Ethnological Significance," *Nature*, 164 (1949), 494–495, p. 494.

68. Lehmann and Raper, "Distribution of the Sickle-Cell Trait in Uganda," 494.

69. Lehmann and Raper, "Distribution of the Sickle-Cell Trait in Uganda," 494.

70. Lehmann and Raper, "Distribution of the Sickle-Cell Trait in Uganda," 494.

71. For some interesting comments on this discourse and practice, see W. MacGaffey, "Concepts of Race in the Historiography of Northeast Africa," *Journal of African History*, 7 (1966), 1–17; P. Harries, "The Roots of Ethnicity: Discourse and the Politics of Language Construction in South-East Africa," *African Affairs*, 87 (1988), 25–52; D. Van Gerven, D. Carlson, and G. Armelagos, "Racial History and Bio-Cultural Adaptation of Nubian Archaeological Populations," *Journal of African History*, 14 (1973), 555–564. See also C. Loring Brace, D. Tracer, L. Yaroch, et al., "Clines and Clusters Versus 'Race': A Test in Ancient Egypt and the Case of a Death on the Nile," *Yearbook of Physical Anthropology*, 36 (1993), 1–31; L. Excoffier, B. Pellegrini, A. Sanchez-Mazas, C. Simon, and A. Langaney, "Genetics and History of sub-Saharan Africa," *Yearbook of Physical Anthropology*, 30 (1987), 151–194.

72. Lehmann and Raper, "Distribution of the Sickle-Cell Trait in Uganda," 494.

73. This debate is still potent today. See C. Loring Brace, D. Tracer, L. Yaroch, et al., "Clines and Clusters Versus 'Race'"; F. Yurco, "Were the Ancient Egyptians Black or White?" *Biblical Archive Review*, 15 (1989), 24–29, 58; M. Bernal, *Black Athena: The Afroasiatic Roots of Classical Civilization*, vol. 1, *The Fabrication of Ancient Greece, 1785–1985* (London, 1987); C. Diop, "Origin of the Ancient Egyptians," in G. Mokhtar (ed.), *General History of Africa II: Ancient Civilizations of Africa* (Berkeley, 1981), 27–51; B. Trigger, "Nubian, Negro, Black, Nilotic," in S. Hochfield and E. Riefstahl (eds.), *Africa in Antiquity: The Arts of Ancient Nubia and the Sudan* (Brooklyn, N.Y., 1978), 26–35. Arguments over the "racial" identity of the ancient Egyptians make a substantial appearance in the eighteenth century, beginning with J. Blumenbach, who observed "three varieties in the national physiognomy of the ancient Egyptians": an "Æthiopian cast," "one approaching to the Hindoo," and one "mixed, partaking in a manner of both of the former" (J. Blumenbach, 1794: 191, quoted by C. Loring Brace, D. Tracer, and A. Yaroch, "Clines and Clusters Versus 'Race,'" 23). Blu-

menbach concluded that "the Egyptian will find his place between the Caucasian and the Æthiopian," with "Æthiopian" being a blanket term for sub-Saharan Africans. By the nineteenth century, a whole generation of racio-craniometric anthropologists picked up on this theme, dutifully considering the possibility of a connection between Egyptians and "Hindoos" (people from the Indian subcontinent). See W. Lawrence, *Lectures on Physiology, Zoology, and the Natural History of Man* (London, 1819); S. Morton, *Crania Ægyptiaca; or Observations on Egyptian Ethnography, Derived from Anatomy, History, and the Monuments* (Philadelphia, 1844); J. Nott, *Two Lectures on the Natural History of the Caucasian and Negro Races* (Mobile, Ala., 1844). J. C. Prichard, for example, sought to explain the "resemblance between the Egyptians and the Hindoos" in terms of a "partial colonization of one country from another." See his *Researches into the Physical History of Mankind*, vol. 2, *Researches into the Physical Ethnography of the African Races*, 4th ed. (London, 1851). This desire to find something "Hindoo" in the Predynastic Egyptians led researchers like Karl Pearson, a physical anthropologist and craniometrist, to propose a bio-quantitative (craniometric) tool for assessing "Hindooness" and the "coefficient of racial likeness" for measuring the "extent" of it. Pearson's coefficient of racial likeness was one of the first quantitative procedures for measuring the admixture proportions, or the proportions which "hybrid" populations derive from their various ancestors. See also Francis Galton's law of ancestral heredity. While these early measures were based on skeletal data, similar techniques are being used for the same purposes in the analyses of human blood group frequencies, abnormal hemoglobins, and other so-called genetic markers. See J. Mielke and M. Crawford (eds.), *Current Development in Anthropological Genetics* (New York, 1980).

74. Seligman, *Races of Africa*, 180.

75. Seligman, *Races of Africa*, 156. However, Seligman is not alone in this. See A. C. Haddon, *The Races of Man* (Cambridge, 1929); and G. W. B. Huntingford, "The Peopling of the Interior of East Africa by its Modern Inhabitants," in R. Oliver and G. Matthew (eds.), *History of East Africa*, vol. 1 (Oxford, 1963), 58–93. Huntingford's is instructive because it is drawing upon sickling—as articulated in the work of none other than Lehmann—in an attempt to substantiate the Hamitic thesis in biological terms (blood). For a timely critique, see J. H. Greenberg, *Studies in African Linguistics Classification* (New Haven, 1955).

76. R. Elsdon-Dew, "Ethnology of Sicklaemia in Uganda," *Nature*, 165 (1950), 763–764, p. 764.

77. Lehmann and Raper, "Distribution of the Sickle-Cell Trait in Uganda," 495.

78. Lehmann and Raper, "Distribution of the Sickle-Cell Trait in Uganda," 494.

79. Lehmann and Raper, "Distribution of the Sickle-Cell Trait in Uganda," 494.

80. H. Lehmann and M. Cutbush, "Sickle-Cell Trait in Southern India," *British Medical Journal*, 1 (1952), 404–405, 404.

81. Lehmann and Cutbush, "Sickle-Cell Trait in Southern India," 404.

82. Lehmann and Cutbush, "Sickle-Cell Trait in Southern India," 404.

83. Lehmann and Cutbush, "Sickle-Cell Trait in Southern India," 404.

84. Lehmann and Cutbush, "Sickle-Cell Trait in Southern India," 404.

85. Lehmann and Cutbush, "Sickle-Cell Trait in Southern India," 404.

86. Lehmann and Cutbush, "Sickle-Cell Trait in Southern India," 404.

87. Lehmann and Cutbush, "Sub-division of Some Southern Indian Communities According to the Incidence of Sickle-Cell Trait and Blood Groups," *Transactions of the Royal Society of Tropical Medicine and Hygiene*, 46 (1952), 380–383; p. 380.

88. Lehmann and Cutbush, "Sub-division of Some Southern Indian Communities," 381.

89. B. S. Guha, "Negrito Racial Strains in India," *Nature*, 121 (1928), 793; and "Negrito Racial Strains in India," *Nature*, 123 (1929), 942–943. While Lehmann and Cutbush established a link between India and East Africa, Guha suggested anthropological connections between India and Melanesia and Australia as all of these places had been shown to have populations with "Negrito" features.

90. Lehmann and Cutbush, "Sub-division of Some Southern Indian Communities," 380.

91. H. Lehmann, "Distribution of the Sickle Cell Gene: A New Light on the Origin of the East Africans," *Eugenics Review*, 46 (1954), 101–121; 109–110.

92. Lehmann and Cutbush, "Sub-division of Some Southern Indian Communities," 382. It is beyond the scope of this work to address the use of sickling as a marker of "race" in India proper; however, the work of Lehmann and Cutbush did spur others to use sickling in addressing India's racial history. See P. K. Sukumaran, L. D. Sanghvi, and G. N. Vyas, "Sickle-Cell Trait in Some Tribes of Western India," *Current Science*, 25 (1956), 290–291; R. N. Shukla and B. R. Solanki, "Sickle-Cell Trait in Central India," *Lancet*, 1 (1958), 297–298; D. K. Sen, "Blood Groups and Haemoglobin Variants in Some Upper Castes of Bengali," *Journal of the Royal Anthropological Institute of Great Britain and Ireland*, 90 (1960), 161–171; R. S. Negi, "The Incidence of Sickle-Cell Trait in Two Bastar Tribes, I," *Man*, 62 (1962), 84–86, and "The Incidence of Sickle-Cell Trait in Bastar, II," *Man*, 63 (1963), 19–21.

93. Lehmann and Cutbush, "Sub-division of Some Southern Indian Communities," 381.

94. Lehmann, "The Sickle-Cell Trait: Not an Essentially Negroid Feature," 9.

95. Lehmann, "The Sickle-Cell Trait: Not an Essentially Negroid Feature," 9.

96. Lehmann, "Distribution of the Sickle Cell Gene," 111.

97. Lehmann, "Distribution of the Sickle Cell Gene," 113, 114, 117, 119, 120.

98. A. C. A. Wright, "Blood Grouping and the Tribal Historian," *Uganda Journal*, 15 (1951), 44–48, p. 44.

99. Wright, "Blood Grouping," 45.

100. Wright, "Blood Grouping," 45.

101. R. Singer, "The Sickle Cell Trait in Africa," *American Anthropologist,* 55 (1953), 634–648, p. 634. This work was followed, one year later, by another which assessed the "origin" of the sickle cell trait. See R. Singer, "The Origin of the Sickle Cell," *South African Journal of Science,* 50 (1954), 287–291.

102. Into the migration-miscegenation camp may be put Wright and Singer, while the following might be placed in the evolution-selection camp: D. R. Swindler, "The Absence of the Sickle Cell Gene in Several Melanesian Societies and Its Anthropological Significance," *Human Biology,* 27 (1955), 284–293; J. Hiernaus, "Physical Anthropology and the Frequency of Genes with a Selective Value: The Sickle Cell Gene," *American Journal of Physical Anthropology,* 13 (1955), 455–472; L. W. Mednick and M. Orans, "The Sickle-Cell Gene: Migration Versus Selection," *American Anthropologist,* 58 (1956), 293–295.

103. A. C. Allison was intellectually close to most if not all the colonial medics whose works are examined here, and he was often their co-investigator in matters of serology, race, and tribes: see A. C. Allison, E. W. Ikin, A. E. Mourant, and A. B. Raper, I: "Blood Groups in Some East African Tribes," *Journal of the Royal Anthropological Institute of Great Britain and Ireland,* 82 (1951–52), 55–59, and II: "Blood Groups of the Amba Pygmoids of Uganda," *Journal of the Royal Anthropological Institute of Great Britain and Ireland* 82 (1951–52), 60–61.

104. A. C. Allison, "Protection Afforded by Sickle-Cell Trait Against Subterian Malarial Infection," *British Medical Journal,* 1 (1954), 290–294; "The Distribution of the Sickle-Cell Trait in East Africa and Elsewhere, and Its Apparent Relationship to the Incidence of Subtertian Malaria," *Transactions of the Royal Society of Tropical Medicine and Hygiene,* 48 (1954), 312–318; "Notes on Sickle-Cell Polymorphism," *Annals of Human Genetics,* 19 (1954), 39–57.

105. Allison, "The Distribution of the Sickle-Cell Trait in East Africa," 314.

106. Allison, "The Distribution of the Sickle-Cell Trait in East Africa," 313.

107. Allison, "The Distribution of the Sickle-Cell Trait in East Africa," 316.

108. Allison, "The Distribution of the Sickle-Cell Trait in East Africa," 316.

109. Frank B. Livingstone, "Anthropological Implications of Sickle Cell Gene Distribution in West Africa," *American Anthropologist,* 60 (1958), 533–562, p. 552.

110. Livingstone, "Anthropological Implications of Sickle Cell Gene Distribution," 556.

111. Frank B. Livingstone, "Who Gave Whom Hemoglobin S: The Use of Restriction Site Haplotype Variation for the Interpretation of the Evolution of the B^s-Globin Gene," *American Journal of Human Biology,* 1 (1989), 289–302, p. 289. In conjunction with Livingstone's a vast literature has emerged, starting in the 1980s, on the use of restriction fragments and sickling. See J. Feldenzer, J. G. Mears, A. L. Burns, et al., "Heterogeneity

of DNA Fragments Associated with the Sickle-Globin Gene," *Journal of Clinical Investigation*, 64 (1979), 751–755; J. Pagnier, J. G. Mears, O. Dunda-Belkhodja, et al., "Evidence for the Multicentric Origin of the Sickle Cell Hemoglobin Gene in Africa," *Proceedings of the National Academy of Science (USA)*, 81 (1984), 1771–1773; R. L. Nagel, "The Origin of the Hemoglobin S Gene: Clinical, Genetic, and Anthropological Consequences," *Einstein Quarterly Journal of Biology and Medicine* (1984), 253–262; A. Ragusa, M. Lombardo, et al., "B^s Gene in Sicily is in Linkage Disequilibrium with the Benin Haplotype: Implications for Gene Flow," *American Journal of Hematology*, 27 (1988), 139–141; S. E. Antonarakis, C. D. Boehm, G. R. Serjeant, et al., "Origin of the B^s-Globin Gene in Blacks: The Contribution of Recurrent Mutation or Gene Conversation or Both," *Proceedings of the National Academy of Science (USA)*, 81 (1984), 853–856; R. L. Nagel, M. E. Fabry, J. Pagnier, et al., "Hematologically and Genetically Distinct Forms of Sickle Cell Anemia in Africa," *New England Journal of Medicine*, 312 (1985), 880–884.

112. Livingstone, "Who Gave Whom Hemoglobin S," 296.

113. A. D. Adekile, "Anthropology of the B^s Gene-flow from West Africa to North Africa, the Mediterranean, and Southern Europe," *Hemoglobin*, 16 (1992), 105–121, p. 118.

Chapter 4. Sickling and the Paradoxes of African American Citizenship

1. L. DeVilbiss, "Sickle Cell Anaemia: Tests for This Little-Known Disease Are Important," *American Mercury*, 89 (July–December 1959), 129–132, p. 130.

2. DeVilbiss, "Sickle Cell Anaemia," 129.

3. DeVilbiss, "Sickle Cell Anaemia," 132.

4. J. Donzelot, *The Policing of Families* (New York, 1979).

5. Foucault's notion of government has since been developed by writers such as G. Burchell, "Liberal Government and Techniques of Self," *Economy and Society*, 22, no. 3 (1993), 267–282; Donzelot, *The Policing of Families*; P. Rabinow, *French Moderns: Norms and Forms of the Social Environment* (Cambridge, 1989); and N. Rose, *Inventing Our Selves: Psychology, Power, and Personhood* (Cambridge, 1996) Rose defines it as "a way of conceptualizing all those more or less rationalized programs, strategies, and tactics for 'the conduct of conduct,' for acting upon the actions of others in order to achieve certain ends . . . In this sense one might speak of the government of a ship, of a family, of a prison or factory, of a colony, and of a nation, as well as of the government of oneself" (12).

6. The programmatic statements made by the proponents of liberal governance universalized the latter to include non-racialized cultures such as the cultures of the poor, the mentally ill, the disabled, women, and other marginalized subjects. I owe this way of formulating the sickling matter to the work of B. Cruikshank, "The Will to Empower: Technologies of Citizenship and the War on Poverty," *Socialist Review*, 23, no. 4 (1994), 29–55.

7. N. Rose, *Governing the Soul: The Shaping of the Private Self* (London, 1990), 6.

8. Rose, *Governing the Soul*, 6.

9. M. Foucault, "Technologies of the Self," in L. H. Martin, H. Gutman, and P. Hutton (eds.), *Technologies of the Self* (Amherst, Mass., 1988), 16–49, p. 18.

10. J. E. Bowman, "Social, Legal and Economic Issues in Sickle Cell Programs," in J. J. Buckley (ed.), *Genetics Now: Ethical Issues in Genetic Research* (Washington, D.C., 1978), 141–171; L. E. Gary, "The Sickle Cell Controversy," *Social Work*, 19, no. 3 (1974), 263–272.

11. "I'm Living on Borrowed Time," *Ebony* (January 1959), 40–46, p. 41.

12. "I'm Living on Borrowed Time," 44.

13. "Incurable 'Negro Disease' Strikes Five in Family: Problems Linked to Sickle Cell Anemia Cloud Life in Upper New York Home," *Ebony*, 21 (May 1966), 154–156, 158, 160, and 162.

14. "Incurable 'Negro Disease' Strikes Five in Family," 162; "Sickle Cell Hits Tar Heel Families" (*Raleigh, N.C.*) *News and Observer* (14 Feb. 1974), p. D12; "Sickle Cell Trait Rampant, But Ineffectual Among Black Footballers, Report Shows," *Chicago Courier* (29 Dec. 1973), p. A11.

15. Rose, *Inventing Our Selves*, 108; see B. Latour, "Visualization and Cognition: Thinking with the Eyes and Hands," *Knowledge and Society: Studies in the Sociology of Culture Past and Present*, 6 (1986), 1–40.

16. Cruikshank, "The Will to Empower," 32.

17. J. C. Lane and R. B. Scott, "Awareness of Sickle Cell Anemia Among Negroes in Richmond, Va.," *Public Health Report*, 84 (1969), 949–953.

18. R. B. Scott, "Health Care Priorities and Sickle Cell Anemia," *Journal of the American Medical Association*, 214, no. 4 (1970), 731–734, p. 731.

19. Scott, "Health Care Priorities," 731.

20. Scott, "Health Care Priorities," 732.

21. Scott, "Health Care Priorities," 732.

22. The notion of disease citizenship is found in the work of the sociologist Talcott Parsons. See his *The Social System* (New York, 1951), 428–479. By the late 1970s, the category of "the cripple"—which echoes the medico-eugenic category of the abnormal or subnormal person—was being contested, first and foremost by activist paraplegics. Eventually it was replaced by the nonmedical, functionalist category of the impaired or disabled person, a terminological shift that coincided with government's acknowledgment of its responsibility toward disabled citizens, who heretofore had relied on philanthropist organizations for support. This acknowledgment resulted in—among many other things—concerted efforts to make public spaces accessible to people in wheelchairs and the development of special education programs. See M. Minow, *Making All the Difference: Inclusion, Exclusion, and American Law* (Ithaca, 1990), 131.

23. Some sickle cell anemia telethons folded in controversy over mismanagement or embezzlement of funds (see *Amsterdam* [*N.Y.*] *News*, July 14, 1973: A7; July 21, 1973: A8, A9, A10; *Philadelphia Inquirer*, July 4, 1973: A6; *Cleveland Press*, March 1, 1973: A11).

24. Scott, "Health Care Priorities," 733.

25. L. Rainwater and W. L. Yancey, *The Moynihan Report and the Politics of Controversy* (Cambridge, Mass., 1967); T. Parsons and K. B. Clark (eds.), *The Negro American* (Boston, 1966); K. B. Clark, *Dark Ghetto: Dilemmas of Social Power* (New York, 1965).

26. Scott, "Health Care Priorities," 734.

27. Scott, "Health Care Priorities," 734.

28. "Incurable 'Negro Disease' Strikes Five in Family," 162.

29. "Sickle Cell Anemia," *Journal of the American Medical Association*, 214, no. 4 (1970), 749.

30. U.S. Congress, Senate. Hearings Before the Subcommittee on Health of the Committee on Labor and Public Welfare, 92nd Cong., 1st sess. (Washington, D.C.: Government Printing Office, 1972), p. 14. Hereafter Hearings.

31. Hearings, 3.

32. See J. S. Haller, *Outcasts from Evolution: Scientific Attitudes of Racial Inferiority, 1859–1900* (Urbana, 1971).

33. Hearings, 62–67.

34. Hearings, 63–64.

35. Hearings, 300.

36. Hearings, 28.

37. Hearings, 82.

38. Hearings, 86.

39. Hearings, 132.

40. In the Tuskegee syphilis study of 1932 to 1972, hundreds of black men who had the disease were monitored by federal researchers but not treated (only told that they had "bad blood"), even as the men went blind and insane. As would be expected, the revelation of this story led to anger and a sort of rhetorical device for grounding talk of medical genocide.

41. Hearings, 18.

42. "The people," Patrick Joyce says, is the "democratic imaginary." P. Joyce, *Democratic Subjects: The Self and the Social in Nineteenth-Century England* (Cambridge, 1994), 5.

43. D. Gregory, "My Answer to Genocide," *Ebony*, 126, no. 12 (1971), 66–72; D. Y. Wilkinson, "For Whose Benefit? Politics and Sickle Cell," *The Black Scholar* (May 1971), 26–31; M. G. Michaelson, "Sickle Cell Anemia: An 'Interesting Pathology,'" *Ramparts*, 10 (1971), 53–58.

44. S. Sontag, *Illness and Its Metaphors* (New York, 1988), is one of the founding texts on disease and signification. Comparing the significations attached to AIDS with those linked to earlier epidemics, she points out that unlike the former with its persistent judgment of the mode of conduct of the individual, "diseases, insofar as they acquired meaning [in the past], were collective calamities, and judgments on a community." Contrary to Sontag, I argue that diseases are always suspended in a web of signification. My reading of sickling in the 1970s follows more closely that of F. Delaporte, *Disease and Civilization: The Cholera in Paris, 1832* (Cambridge, 1986). Thus, I do not accept the idea of a nondiscursive space where something as disease can have meaning. The issue then is not the nature of reality but the use of significations.

45. These databases constituted, I argue, a technology of inscription defining, as Mark Poster has pointed out, "positionalities of subjects according to its rules of formation." M. Poster, "Databases as Discourse, or Electronic Interpellations," in P. Heelas, S. Lash, and P. Morris (eds.), *Detraditionalization: Critical Reflections on Authority and Identity* (London, 1996), 277–293.

46. I am interested in the claim that the government's sickling prevention program was a failure first, because this idea was central to the discourses defining sickling in the mid- and late 1970s, and, second, because the notion of failure, as seen in the discussion of the Moynihan Report, was a highly productive element in the dominant discourse on— or representation of—the black community at the time. Screening for the prevention of sickling was commonly compared with, for example, the screening program for Tay-Sachs, which was carried out around the same time and which was generally considered a success. But the population targeted by the Tay-Sachs screening program—Baltimore's Ashkenazi Jewish community—these critics readily point out, tended to be well educated, middle class, and close knit. The implied argument then was that the sickling prevention program failed because it targeted a population with the diametrically opposite characteristics, that is, an uneducated and poor community in general disarray. See P. Reilly, *Genetics, Law, and Social Policy* (Cambridge, 1977), 29–33.

47. See B. Latour, *Science in Action* (London, 1987); and N. Rose, "Calculable Minds and Manageable Individuals," *History of the Human Sciences*, 1 (1988), 179–200.

48. It would be tempting to establish uniformity between the articulation of "black genocide" here and that tied to the family and population control policy of the 1960s and 1970s, and even today around the issues of AIDS and drugs. A history of these forms of agency and resistance in the black community has yet to be written. For my purposes here genocide is positioned by discourse, suggesting that something new is always addressed in terms of something old.

49. M. Foucault, "The Politics of Health in the Eighteenth Century," in C. Gordon (ed.), *Power/Knowledge: Selected Interviews and Other Writings, 1972–1977* (New York, 1980).

Coda

1. Italo Calvino, *Mr. Palomar*, trans. William Weaver (San Diego, 1985), 81.

2. Calvino, *Mr. Palomar*, 82.

3. Calvino, *Mr. Palomar*, 83.

4. Calvino's story brings to mind the first two chapters of Claude Lévi-Strauss's *Elementary Structures of Kinship*.

5. Italo Calvino, *Mr. Palomar*, 81.

Acknowledgments

Because this book has been so long in the making, it is impossible to acknowledge individually all those friends, colleagues, and antagonists who over the years have asked provocative questions and made helpful comments in response to presentations of ideas that eventually found their way into the manuscript.

The seed for the book was planted while I was a graduate student at the University of Connecticut, splitting my time between medical anthropology and a program in economy and society. James C. Faris supervised my dissertation which, in summary fashion, was a polemic with the adaptationist thesis of disease. He, along with Scott Cook and Ben Magubane, taught me how to carry out critical and political analyses of disease and to problematize the pervasive instrumentalist knowledge and practice of anthropology.

I thank Naja Fuglsang-Damgaard for putting up with my syntax, vocabulary, and hopeless polemics for longer than she would like to remember. Over the years she has taken on the realization of this project as her own, and while I may have introduced her to the anthropology of medicine and genetics, she has taught me how to write effectively about these matters.

I also thank the following people who, at one point or another, read the manuscript and offered helpful suggestions: Lisa Moore, Subashree Rangaswami, James Sidbury, Kathleen Stewart, and Benigno Trigo. I am especially grateful to Ira Buchler, who generously shared with me his knowledge of Foucault and was most helpful in bringing to the surface many of the ideas presented here. For their friendship and support, I thank Bob Fernea, Ward Keeler, and Sam Wilson.

Finally, I thank the anonymous readers of the manuscript for their insightful criticism and advice; Noreen O'Connor for her superlative copyediting; and Patricia Smith for supporting the manuscript since the first time it crossed her desk. Her enthusiasm has made it a pleasure to publish with the University of Pennsylvania Press.

My research has been supported most generously by the National Science Foundation, the Ford Foundation, which gave me a postdoctoral grant and hence a year to radically rethink an earlier draft, and the Graduate School and the Center for African and African American Studies at the University of Texas.

*   *   *

Earlier versions of two chapters were previously published: Chapter 1 in *Comparative Studies in Society and History* (1995); Chapter 2 in *Social History of Medicine* (1997). I thank these journals for permission to publish these revised pieces. A preliminary version of Chapter 3 was presented to the conference "New Directions in Kinship Study: A Core Concept Revisited," sponsored by the Wenner-Gren Foundation. I thank the Foundation and the participants for helpful suggestions.

Index

Aaron, Henry (Black Athletes Foundation), 117–18
Adekile, A. D., 91
Admixture: and sickling, 18–19, 24, 26–27, 53; and the Negro, 30, 33; "disadvantages" of, 35, 92, 138 n.52, 139 n.62; indexing of, 49–50. *See also* Hamitic thesis; Hybridity
Africa: as "obscure" social environment, 75; as primordial reality, 59, 77; ethnic composition of, 48, 64; racial link with southern India, 81–85
African Americans: and citizenship, 94–95, 106, 109–11, 119, 122; as a target of governance, 96, 104–7; government neglect of, 94–95, 108–10; new political subjectivity of (1970s), 96, 101; sickle cell anemia as a problem specific to, 104; social responsibility of, 95, 100–101
African body: anemia and, 66, 73, 144 n.835, 146 n.61; norm for, 73; vs. the diasporic African body, 59. *See also* Colonial medicine
African Negroes: vs. American Negroes, 63. *See also* "True" Negroes
Africans: Bantu, 76–78; construction of as populations, 56–57; Nilotes, 76–77. *See also* Hamites
Agency, 8
Ahmann, C., 48, 140 n.77

AIDS, 10–11
Allen, Garland E., 40
Allison, A. C., 87–88
Alpines, 26
American Mercury, 92, 96
American Negroes: and anthropathology, 30–32; as biogenetic category, 41; as hybrids, 3, 34–35; as objects of knowledge, 29; biogenetic differences among, 46–47; internal differentiation of, 134 n.15, 139 n.64; pathologization of, 29–30, 34, 134 n.7; vs. Africans within Africa, 63; "whitening" (or "bleaching") of, 30
"American people," 26–27
American Red Cross: blood policy of, 92
Anderson, Elmer, 116–17
Anemias: classification of, and race, 14; congenital hemolytic icterus, 14; hemolytic jaundice, 14; von Kaksch's, 14. *See also* Sickle cell anemia
Anthropathology, 44; 135 n.20; defined, 31
Anthropology: and DuBois, 34; biological, and sickling, 5, 34, 42; medical, 36, 130 n.25; New Physical, 138 n.46; racialist, 18, 23, 39–40, 42, 45, 90, 138 n.47; serological, 30. *See also* Ethnology
Archibald, R. G., 17
Ashman, Richard, 51–54

Balovale district (Northern Rhodesia):
as an ethnological laboratory, 66;
described, 65–66; distribution of
sickle cell anemia in, 66–67; ethno-
statistical profile of sickling in, 68;
"tribal" history of, 69–71
Bantu. See Africans
Bauer, Julius, 39
Beckles, Frank, 112, 117
Beet, E. A., 35, 58, 64–76
Berbers. See Hamites
Bibb, J., 48
Biology: molecular, 40; molecular, and
sickling, 4–5, 90–91
Biomedicine, 55
Black Athletes Foundation, 117–18
Black community: as a target of gover-
nance, 106–7, 110, 114–24; Moyni-
han Report (1965) on, 105, 117;
Robert B. Scott on, 105
Blackness, 48; as a principle of alliance,
101
Blacks. See African Americans
Blood: Hamitic, 49, 63; Hamitic, and
sickling, 77, 79–80; Negro, 92; purity
of, 55; rhesus antigens (Ro(cDe)),
81–82; rhesus incompatibility, 52;
symbolics of, 55–56, 75, 90, 141 n.5;
Veddian (or Veddoid), 84–85
Blood groups: and race, 30–31, 45
British Medical Journal, 35
British South Africa Company (BSAC),
69
Brown, Gordon G., 71–72
Bruce-Miller (District Commissioner),
69–70

Calvino, Italo, 125
Canguilhem, Georges, 128 n.12, 131
n.12
Caribs: Black, of Honduras, 42–44, 139
n.58
Castana, V., 16
Cerebral palsy: public image of, 103–4
Childhood diseases: dreaded, 94, 96
Citizenship: and African Americans,
94–95; and personal responsibility,
95

Clarke, F., 25
Clay, William, 115
Clinic: as site of medical knowledge
production, 15
Colonial administration: fusion with
ethnology and medicine, 69–73, 75.
See also Indirect rule
Colonial medicine, 143 n.21; and sick-
ling, 61–62; and the African body,
56–57; fusion with ethnology, 62, 75,
144 n.29, 145 n.60
Committee on the Negro, 29
Community. See Black community
Comparative studies: critique of, 10–11
Consciencization, 9
Contamination: of social body, 27
Cook, Jerome, 10
Cooley, T. B., 14–15, 19, 21, 27, 38, 40,
58–60
Cuba: as "racial melting pot," 18, 132
n.24
Culturalism, 34, 135 n.18
Culture: defined, 9
Cutbush, Marie, 81–85
Cystic fibrosis: public image of, 103–4

Darwinism, 54; social, 29–30
Degeneracy: biogenetic, 35; constitu-
tional, 39, 134 n.7. See also Hybridity
Delaporte, François, 128 n.12
DeVilbiss, Lydia A., 92–93
Diggs, Lemuel W., 48, 50, 54
Discourse networks, 5–6, 8–9, 131 n.5
Discourse network analysis, 6–11, 127
n.9
Disease: and race, 2, 12–14, 30–31; and
signification, 153 n.44; as technology
of governance, 96; "black-related,"
2–3, 16; racial versus social, 134
n.17; versus health, 137 n.34; versus
illness, 7. See also Childhood diseases
Donzelot, Jacques, 59, 93
DuBois, W. E. B., 32–34; and anthropology, 34, 134 nn.16–17

East African Medical Journal, 35, 61
East African: racial link between the
Veddoid and, 83–85

Ebony Magazine, 97, 99, 106
Egypt: as a zone of racial mixture, 78
Egyptians (ancient): racial identity of,
    147 n.73. *See also* Hamites
Eickstedt, E. von, 83
Ellison, Ralph, 12, 26
Elsdon-Dew, R., 79
Emmel, Victor E. 1, 10, 15
Epstein, P., 58
Erythroblastosis fetalis, 51–52
Ethnicity: as ideological category, 3
Ethnology: fusion with colonial ad-
    ministration, 69–73; fusion with
    genetics, 42; fusion with medicine,
    36, 44–45, 60, 66–67, 74–75, 86, 145
    n.60; defined, 136 n.26
Eugenics, 38–40, 42, 51, 54; modern
    synthesis, 51; reform, 40
Evans, R. W., 61
Evolution (social), 77
Experience: personal, 8–9

Figlio, K., 128n.9
Fisher, L. J., 39
Foucault, Michel, 8, 23, 55–56, 74–75,
    94–95, 99, 128 n.12, 131 n.5
Fouche, H. H., 46
Frazier, E. F., 47

Galton, Francis, 51. *See also* Eugenics;
    Genetics
Genealogy: and race, 18, 23, 25–26
Genetics: and sickling, 5, 42; animal,
    52; clinical, 34; Galtonian, 57, 75;
    human (modern), and race, 40, 46,
    142 n.12; population, and sickling, 5,
    74–75
Genetic information: and full citizen-
    ship, 122
Genetic screening (for the sickle cell
    trait), 105–6, 113, 122, 154 n.45; as
    discriminatory practice, 118, 120–22
German, W. M., 42–44, 54
Gilman, Sander L., 2–3
Giorgio, Anthony, 118
Good, B., 130 n.25
Gordon, M., 52
Governance. *See* Government

Government: and inscription, 95–96;
    and isolation, 95–96; defined, 151
    n.5; liberal discourse of (1970s), 94;
    sickling as technology of, 96; the
    "black community" as an effect of,
    106–7. *See also* Personal responsibility
Graham, G. S., 12, 14–15, 19–20, 38–39
Grant, Madison, 26–27
Greeks: as prototypically white, 19;
    in Western European discourse on
    Europeanness, 132 n.26; sickling in,
    4, 26, 85
Greenwald, Louis, 16, 24–25
Guha, B. S., 83

Haddon, A. C., 78
Haldane, J. B. S., 51–52
Haller, John S., 29
Hamites, 49, 63, 76–77, 88
Hamitic thesis, 63, 77–79, 81–82, 88,
    90
Health and Physique of the Negro American
    (W. E. B. DuBois), 32–33
Henderson, Deborah L., 30
Herrick, James B., 1, 10, 37
Herskovits, Melville, 50
Higham, J., 26
Hirst, Paul, 9, 129
Hirszfeld, Hanna, 30
Hirszfeld, Ludwik, 30
Hodges, John D., 47–51, 54
Hrdlicka, Ales, 29
Human Genetic Diversity Project,
    10–11, 142 n.12
Hutt, Bruce A., 71–72
Hybridity (hybridization): and disease,
    3–4, 34–35, 42, 46, 48–49, 52, 128
    n.9, 134 n.7, 138 n.52, 140 n.79. *See
    also* Admixture; Hamitic thesis
Hygiene: defined, 104

Iliffe, J., 60
Illness: versus disease, 7, 130 n.25
India (southern): racial link with
    Africa, 81–85; Veddids (or Ved-
    doids), 82–83
Indirect rule, 60, 142 n.13

Inquiries into Human Faculty (Francis Galton), 51
Interbreeding. *See* Admixture; Hybridity
Intermarriage, 42, 44. *See also* Admixture; Hybridity
Italians: sickling in, 16, 26, 75, 85. *See also* Sicilians

Jews (ideological construct versus "real" people), 3
Johnson, Lyndon B., 105
Joseph, H. W., 15
Journal of the American Medical Association, 107

Kennedy, Edward M., 112–13, 115–18
Kevles, Daniel J., 40
Kittler, Friedrich A., 5–6, 131 n.5
Kleinman, Arthur, 8–9
Korb, J. G., 15

Laboratory: as site of medical knowledge production, 15, 32, 131 n.12
Lancet, 35
Lane, J. C., 102
Latour, B., 123–24
Lawrence, J. S., 17–18
Leakey, L. S., 85
Lee, P. 15, 19, 21, 38, 40, 58–60
Lehmann, H., 36, 58, 76–85, 146 n.65
Lévi-Strauss, Claude, 88
Lewanika (Lozi "chief"), 69
Lewis, Jerry ("Jerry's Kids"), 103
Lewis, Julian H., 30–32, 34, 44
Little, C. C., 52
Livingstone, F. B., 88–90
Lunda people, 69–71, 73, 145 n.45
Luvale people, 69–71, 73, 145 n.45

Malaria: sickling as evolutionary response to, 87–89
Mason, Verne, 1, 13–14
McBride, David, 12–13, 130 n.1
McCarty, S. H., 15, 19–20, 38–39
McGavack, T. H., 42–44, 54
Medic, 135 n.21

Medicine: and the formation of the Negro as an object of knowledge, 29–30; clinical, 130 n.25; clinical, and sickling, 4; constitutional, 38; fusion with ethnology, 36, 60, 66–67, 86, 145 n.60. *See also* Colonial medicine
Mediterraneans, 26
Meinhof, C., 78
Mexicans: sickling in, 24, 26
Meyer, J., 10
Mitchell, Accie, 116
Mitchell, Philip, 71–72
Miscegenation. *See* Admixture; Hamitic thesis; Hybridity
Miyamoto, K., 15
Mongrelization, 27
Moynihan Report: and the black community, 105, 112, 119
Mulattos, 26; "passing" as white, 23
Muscular dystrophy: public image of, 103–4

National Association for the Advancement of Colored People (NAACP), 109
National Institutes of Health, 112–13
National Research Council, 29
National Sickle Cell Anemia Prevention Act: statements of, 110–11; versus National Sickle Cell Control Act, 93–94, 109, 114–15
National Urban League, 109, 114
Nature, 76
Neel, James V., 35, 39–40, 42, 45–46, 51, 74, 139 n.62
Negro: usage of term explained, 133 n.1
Negro Family: The Case for National Action, The (Moynihan Report), 105
New York Times, 26
Nilotes. *See* Africans
Nixon, Richard (President), 108–9, 113, 120
Nordics, 26
Northern Rhodesia. *See* Balovale District

Ogden, M. A., 25
Osborne, Thomas, 7, 130 n.25

Packard, R., 58
Papstein, R., 69–70
Passing of the Great Race (Madison Grant), 26
Paul, Diane B., 40
Pauling, Linus, 39
Personal responsibility: as a technology of government, 94–95, 100–101
Physiognomy: and race, 20–21, 23
Pincus, J. B., 18, 21–23
Pollock, Griselda, 14
Population: as mode of visualization, 74; as technology of power, 55–57, 68, 74–75
Power, 55–56, 124; modern, 55; pre-modern, 55
Progress, 77
Puerto Ricans: sickling in, 24, 26

Race: and classification of anemias, 14; and heredity, 12–14; and identity, 20–21; and physiognomy, 18, 20–21, 23; and purity, 18, 59; and scientific discourse, 139 n.63; and sickling, 16; and susceptibility to disease, 30–31; anthropological construction of, 18; as ideological category, 3, 128 n.11, 139 n.63, 147 nn. 71, 73; as socioeconomic phenomenon, 96; biochemical index of, 30; genetic determination of, 3, 13; "majority," 53; "minority," 53; sickling as marker of, 39; sickling as symptom of, 39. *See also* Racial formalism; Racialism; Racism
Races of Africa, The (C. G. Seligman), 78
Racial formalism, 33–34. *See also* Race; Racialism; Racism
Racial history, 77
Racialism, 26, 135 n.18. *See also* Race; Racial formalism; Racism
Racism: and the symbolics of blood, 56
Raper, Alan B., 36–37, 41–42, 44–46, 54, 58, 76–80, 84, 86, 90

Rationalism (classic), 6
Research Foundation for Sickle Cell Anemia, 109, 116–17
Rising Tide of Color Against White World Supremacy, The, 26
Risk: in sickling, 94
Roberts, Kenneth, 27
Rose, Nikolas, 6, 95, 101, 121, 123
Rosenfeld, S., 18, 21–23

Saturday Evening Post, 26–27
Scientific epidemiology, 12–13
Scott, Robert B., 102–7, 119
Scott, Roland B. (Howard), 115
Seligman, C. G., 49, 78–79, 81, 85
Senate hearings: as inscriptive devices, 112
Sexuality: "analytics" of, 55, 74
Sicilians: sickling in, 4, 85
Sickle cell anemia: and admixture, 47–54; differential distribution of among Africans and African Americans, 34–37, 40–41, 46; illness narratives of, 97–100; incidence in African Americans, 47; relation with sickle cell trait, 35, 37–40, 42, 44; representation during Senate hearings on sickling, 112
Sickle cell trait: and "government through the family," 93; and the making of a "normal" African body, 73; and the reproductive behavior of African Americans, 106; as norm for Negroes, 40; differential distribution of among Africans and African Americans, 35–36, 40–41; differential distribution within the African continent, 63; genetic definition, 5; genetic screening for, 105–6, 111–21; incidence in African Americans, 46–47, 127 n.8; in the National Sickle Cell Anemia Prevention Act, 111; relation with anemia, 35, 37–40, 42, 44, 74, 137 n.34; representation during Senate hearings on sickling, 112; social responsibility of carriers, 100
Sicklemia, 38, 60

Sickling: defined, 1; "active," 38; and citizenship, 3–4; and hybridity, 3–4, 49, 52; and job and insurance discrimination, 122; and malaria, 87–88; and natural selection, 87, 140 n.77; and race, 15–16; and social responsibility, 100; and thalassemia, 27; and the assessment of racial kinship, 76; and the identification of racial origins, 81; and the "informed (procreational) choice," 100; and the naturalization of tribes, 3–4; and the rewriting of tribal histories, 70–71, 79–80; and the "sick person," 98–99, 130 n.27; and venereal disease, 93; and whiteness, 3–4; as "black-related" disease, 2–3, 16, 23, 24, 35; 100–101; as discursive effect, 6; as dreaded disease of childhood, 96, 102–3; as manageable disease, 93; as marker of race, 2, 39, 76; as public health issue, 92, 104; as site of government intervention, 101–2, 106; as object of government neglect, 108–10, 121; as symptom of race, 2, 39; "failure" of government prevention program for, 122–23, 154 n.46; heterozygotes vs. homozygotes, 74; in African Americans (1930s), 136 n.24; in Africa versus the United States, 36–37; in clinical medicine, 4; in genetics, 5, 74, 138 n.43; in molecular biology, 4, 138 n.43; in South America, 136 n.25; in Uganda, 76–77; in "whites," 20, 22, 24–26; "latent," 15, 38; mandatory premarital testing for, 92–93; narratives of, 101; prevention and control, 93–94, 100, 106; public image, 103; telethons for, 103–4, 152 n.23
Singer, R., 86–87
Sleeping sickness, 145 n.60
Social sciences: and medicine, 2
Sociomedical racialism, 12–13
Southern Europeans: "misdiagnosis" of, 27; sickling in, 26. See also Greeks; Italians; Sicilians

Speciation: human, 53–54
Spickard, P. R., 23
"Status degenerativus," 39–40, 137 n.40
Stepan, Nancy L., 40
Stewart, W. B., 17–19, 23
Stoddard, L., 26
Subjectivism, 7
Subjectivity, 7–8, 129 n.21; (African American) as an instrument of government, 96. See also Black community
"Subnormal individual," 38–40
Switzer, P. K., 46, 139 n.64
Sydenstricker, V. P., 15–16, 38
Syphilis, 38

Technologies of the self, 97, 99, 101
Thalassemia, 27
Transactions of the Royal Society of Tropical Medicine and Hygiene, 35
"Tribal twenties," 26
Tribes, 144 n.30; as effects of colonial administration, 60, 68, 142 n.13; as unit of colonial medical analysis, 144 n.29; naturalization of, 57, 60, 72–73, 78
Trowell, H. C., 36, 58, 61–64
"True Negroes," 49, 78; defined, 63
Tuberculosis, 12–13
Tunney, John V., 115

Uganda Journal, 85
United States: as an "anthropological laboratory," 32, 59

Vaughan, Megan, 57–58, 66
Veddids. See India

Wartofsky, M. W., 128 n.9
White, C. M. N. (District Officer of Balovale), 70–71
Whiteness: "apparently white" individuals, 18–19, 21–24, 28, 138 n.53; criteria for, 23, 26–27, 138 n.53. See also Mulattos; Greeks; Italians; Sicilians

Wiener, A. S., 51–52
Williams, Richard, 2
Woolley, Penny, 9
Wright, A. C. A., 85–86

Zambesi River: as an administrative
    border, 70
Zapp, John, 113